NATE

Reading Words

A commentary on key terms
in the teaching of reading

Barry Stierer and David Bloome

Reading Words is published by the National Association for the Teaching of English (NATE), the UK subject teacher association for all aspects of the teaching of English from pre-school to university.

NATE
50 Broadfield Road
Broadfield Business Centre
Sheffield S8 OXJ
Tel: 0 114 255 5419
Fax: 0 114 255 5296

ISBN 0 901291 38 2

© NATE and authors 1994

First published 1994

Cover design by Barry Perks Graphic Design.
Printed in the United Kingdom by York Publishing Services, 64 Hallfield Road, Layerthorpe, York, Y03 7XQ.

A definition of language is always, implicitly or explicitly, a definition of human beings in the world. The received categories – 'world', 'reality', 'nature', 'human', – may be counterposed or related to the category 'language', but it is now commonplace to observe that all categories, including the category 'language', are themselves constructions in language and can thus only with an effort, and within a particular system of thought, be separated from language for relational inquiry. Such efforts and such systems, nevertheless, constitute a major part of the history of thought.

Raymond Williams (1977)
Marxism and literature
Oxford: Oxford University Press, p. 21

THE AUTHORS

Barry Stierer lives in Brighton. He is a Staff Tutor at the Open University, dividing his time between the Open University's regional office in East Grinstead and its headquarters in Milton Keynes, where he is a member of the Centre for Language and Communication in the School of Education. He contributes to the Open University's programme of distance-education courses in the field of language and literacy in education, and conducts research on classroom literacy activities. He has worked in nursery schools, primary schools and in adult education. Prior to joining the Open University in 1990 he worked at Roehampton Institute, the University of Bristol and the University of London Institute of Education. Recent publications include a critique of Martin Turner's pamphlet *Sponsored Reading Failure*, ('Simply doing their job? The politics of reading standards and real books', in *Language Matters*, 1990/1 No. 3, pp. 2–8) and two edited volumes: *Language, literacy and learning in educational practice* (co-edited with Janet Maybin) and *Researching language and literacy in social context* (co-edited with David Graddol and Janet Maybin), both published by Multilingual Matters, 1994.

David Bloom lives in Amherst, Massachusetts. He is a Professor in the Reading and Writing Program in the School of Education at the University of Massachusetts at Amherst. A former secondary English teacher, elementary school teacher and reading specialist, he currently teaches post-graduate courses in the teaching of reading and writing, reading and writing difficulties, and research on reading, writing, language and literacy. He taught previously at Cleveland State University and at the University of Michigan. His publications include three edited books: *Literacy and schooling* (1987), *Classrooms and literacy* (1989) and *Alternative perspectives on assessing children's language and literacy* (with Kathleen Holland and Judith Solsken, 1994), all published by Ablex, and book chapters and journal articles on reading and writing as social and linguistic processes. He is the co-editor of *Linguistics and Education: An International Research Journal.*

ACKNOWLEDGEMENTS

We are fortunate to have friends and colleagues, on both sides of the Atlantic, who were willing to read and critique early drafts of this book. We are pleased to acknowledge their help: Bess Altwerger, Myra Barrs, Jon Davison, Ann Egan-Robertson, Yetta Goodman, Harold Rosen, Patrick Shannon and Alastair West. We were also fortunate to receive feedback from students, mostly practising teachers, who were taking post-graduate courses in Reading and Writing at Smith College in Northampton, Massachusetts, and at the University of Massachusetts in Amherst, Massachusetts. We have tried to incorporate the suggestions they made, build on the strengths they saw and address the weaknesses they identified. Any of the book's merits are due in good measure to their assistance; the flaws that remain are our responsibility alone.

During this project we have been especially gratified by our association with NATE. We would like to acknowledge the support of Angel Scott who, as NATE Publications Officer, helped guide the book through the publication process, providing helpful feedback and encouragement along the way. We are also very grateful to the NATE Publications Committee for backing this project from the outset and for agreeing to include the book in its list of publications.

Finally, we greatly appreciate the support of the Open University, the University of Massachusetts at Amherst, the University of Sussex and the US–UK Fulbright Commission. Their financial support made it possible for us to collaborate. The views and opinions expressed in this book do not necessarily represent the views or policies of the Open University, the University of Massachusetts at Amherst, the University of Sussex or the US–UK Fulbright Commission, and they do not necessarily represent the views and opinions of the friends, colleagues and students listed above.

CONTENTS

INTRODUCTION

This book is a commentary on the vocabulary used to talk about the teaching of reading. We've selected some of the more widely used terms and tried to unpack the meanings, assumptions and uses associated with them. Although we have organised the book as a series of discrete entries, the book is more than an analysis of individual words. Taken together, the entries provide a broader commentary on the language of the teaching of reading. We hope it will lead teachers and researchers to a more vigorous discussion and reflection on the nature of reading and teaching reading, and on the role of language in influencing ideas and actions.

Background

When we were learning to become teachers and taking courses on the teaching of reading in the mid-1970s, there were many technical terms to learn, and ordinary words were often given special definitions. The terms we were asked to learn – like *code, comprehension, readiness, remedial reading* – were presented as having exact and single definitions. It was our job to learn their meanings. Neither the terms, nor the information about the teaching of reading which they encoded, were presented to us as being problematical or open to question.

Our experiences as teachers in primary and secondary schools, and our later experiences in teacher education and as reading researchers, led us to question what we had been taught about reading. Like many teachers and researchers we began to suspect that the terms we had learned were more problematical than we had originally thought. It was not just that the definitions we had been taught seemed inaccurate or misleading. It seemed to us and others that there was not, and there might not be, a single stable definition for these key terms. More importantly, we began to suspect that the more widely used terms in the teaching of reading were having subtle but powerful influences on how teachers were thinking about reading and how they were teaching reading. We found it especially disturbing that these widely used terms, whose meanings were largely taken for granted, seemed to embody complex theories, values and assumptions that we found difficult to accept and at odds with our experiences.

As a result we, like many other people, tried to avoid using these problematical terms in our work and in our discussions with colleagues. When we did use them we did so with implied quotation marks (and real quotation marks when using the terms in our writing). We sometimes sought substitute terms that might communicate more accurately what we thought, as well as our displeasure with the terms they were replacing. We used 'early reading' and 'early literacy' instead of 'readiness'; we used 'miscue' instead of 'error'; and we used 'strategies' instead of 'skills'. However, we did not fully articulate why we felt that the more prevalent terms were problematical, or how these terms functioned within the profession. Part of the reason why it was difficult to articulate this was because the field was overwhelmingly concerned with effectiveness, and with technical improvements. There seemed to be no forum, and no language, for a critical examination of the fundamental terms in the teaching of reading.

During the 1980s, new conceptual frameworks were being developed which located reading in the broader context of literacy. A number of models were constructed which did not rely on a single definition of reading or of literacy. Instead, they viewed reading as a broad range of social and cultural practices, metaphors, political interests and ideologies. There were also new approaches being developed for examining language, based on theories of discourse, which linked everyday uses of language with the way power is exercised in a range of contexts. The concepts, as well as the analytical tools, were emerging which could enable the kind of examination of terminology in the teaching of reading which had previously evaded us.

The two of us got to know each other during the academic year 1992–93, which David spent in Britain as a Visiting Fulbright Scholar at the University of Sussex. Apart from discovering that we shared a great deal in common in our professional histories, we found that, for quite different reasons, we were each searching for a publication which unpacked the dominant terminology for the teaching of reading, in a way which was consistent with our own theoretical and methodological outlook. David was writing a book on assessing and addressing reading and writing difficulties, in which he was attempting to broaden the perspectives used in understanding reading and writing difficulties. Barry was involved in producing a new module on language and literacy in the Open University's distance-learning MA in Education. He wished to include in the set reading for the course an article which applied some of the new ideas about reading and literacy on the one hand, and discourse analysis on the other, to the specialised vocabulary for the teaching of reading. This would enable practitioners taking the course to see how these insights could be used to gain a deeper understanding of the language they used in their own work. Despite our best efforts, we could not find a publication which achieved what we needed. Several dictionaries of technical terms were available, and several major dictionary and encyclopedia projects had been recently undertaken. But these publications did not approach the subject from the critical perspectives we had in mind. We therefore resolved to try and write the thing ourselves, and this book is the result.

Theoretical influences

It is traditional in scholarly monographs to discuss the theoretical framework that guided the study. Usually, the discussion recounts the books, journal articles and academic discussions that influenced the authors. Our work on this book *has* been influenced by academic sources, but it has also been influenced by our experiences as teachers, teacher educators and researchers working in primary and secondary classrooms. We view these experiences and our conversations with teachers, parents and pupils as important theoretical influences, and throughout this book we make heavy use of them.

We knew from our experiences working in classrooms that the meanings of key terms in the teaching of reading were often more complicated than what was written in technical dictionaries. We also knew that certain words in the teaching of reading – like 'phonics' and 'whole language' – were the sites of much debate and argument. These debates had real consequences. Teachers and pupils were often labelled by these words: Ms Smith is a 'real books' teacher; Ms Jones is a 'phonics' person; Stephen is a 'remedial' reader; John is 'dyslexic'. The labels had real consequences for the opportunities teachers and pupils had, and for how their behaviour was interpreted.

In addition to our experiences in classrooms, there have been a number of scholarly works that have helped us to articulate a critical examination of the vocabulary of the teaching of reading. Two different but related fields of scholarship have been especially influential on our work here. The first consists of studies in language and ideology, and the second consists of studies of the social construction of reading and literacy. Part of what brings these two fields together is their interest in revealing the ideologies behind everyday language and literacy practices, including those that occur in classrooms.

Language and ideology

The first body of theoretical work which has strongly influenced us in our thinking about this project is scholarship which has examined the relationship between language in use (or discourse) and the exercise of power. The field of critical discourse analysis offered us two related theoretical tools: first, a set of ideas which helped to explain the way in which the vocabulary used in the teaching of reading is linked to wider power relationships; and second, a practical method for unpacking this vocabulary in a way which located it in its contexts of use.

Explanatory ideas

The first tool, the explanatory ideas, appealed to us because they related to our starting point: that the more widely used terms in the teaching of reading – which can often seem so neutral and innocuous – contain, and at the same time transmit, an implicit set of values, assumptions and definitions. These have real consequences for teachers' thinking and practice, and for the educational experience of children in school. Moreover, they are related to powerful interests in education and society. Our starting point was therefore a recognition that the dominant vocabulary in reading pedagogy is *ideological* – that is, it is an example of:

> an implicit philosophy in the practical activities of social life, backgrounded and taken for granted, that connects it to common sense.
>
> *(Fairclough, 1989, p. 84)*

Our conceptual framework drew from a wide range of work in the area of discourse analysis and critical language study. It would be inappropriate to review that work comprehensively here, but some of the more influential sources are listed in the Bibliography at the end of this Introduction. The key explanatory idea for us from these theories of discourse is that language plays a central role in power relations and in the exercise of ideology. According to these theories, discourse works ideologically in at least three ways:

•   Discourse positions members of social groups. That is, the language does not just reflect people's relationships to each other, it helps to construct the position of the people involved in the discourse – for example as active or passive, or as central or marginal.

•   Discourse constitutes and sustains institutional relationships. That is, language itself serves as a vehicle through which institutions (like schools, for example) maintain hierarchies of power.

•   Discourse appeals to common sense. That is, the language itself achieves a curiously neutral quality which obscures its own ideological underpinnings. This often has the effect of reducing ambiguity and multiple meanings to a single, taken-for-granted meaning, and positions any alternative use of discourse as marginal and nonsensical. Fairclough puts it thus:

> Ideology is most effective when its workings are least visible. If one becomes aware that a particular aspect of common sense is sustaining power inequalities at one's own expense, it ceases to be common sense, and may cease to have the capacity to sustain power relations, i.e. it ceases to function ideologically.
>
> *(Fairclough, 1989, p.85)*

Practical approach to language study

The other theoretical tool offered by this work on language and ideology is a practical approach for analysing spoken and written language in a range of social contexts – from immediate interactive contexts (like classrooms), to institutional contexts (like schools), to wider societal contexts (like the political and cultural constraints within which schools operate). Since our aim was to scrutinise a particular kind of language which is an integral part of these different levels of social context, and to try to do so systematically, this work offered an approach well-suited to our purpose.

Norman Fairclough and his colleagues at the University of Lancaster have formulated a detailed procedure for analysing discourse and discursive practices, which they call *critical language study*. This involves an examination of discourse at the level of vocabulary, of grammar and of sustained text. This is not to say that we can simply 'read off' meaning from certain language forms. But identifying these key features of the language is an important start in the process of interpreting and explaining the way language functions ideologically in specific contexts. More detailed explanations of this method, and its underlying rationale, can be found in Fairclough (1989) and Clark *et al.* (1988).

We have found that focusing closely on certain linguistic features of the discourse of reading pedagogy has been especially productive. We discuss some of these features below.

Nominalisations. Nominalisations are processes which have been converted into nouns. The discourse of reading pedagogy contains a number of terms which are nominalised forms of processes, often using suffixes such as -ment, -tion or -sion, -ity and -ness. Fairclough argues that nominalisation is a form of reductionism, in the sense that crucial aspects of the process are left unspecified. For example, in transforming a verb into a noun, its *tense* is lost, so there is no indication of the timing of the process. Similarly, *modality* is eliminated, so that the relationships between people involved in the process have been obscured. And *agency* is hidden, so that the instigator of the process in question is only implied.

Thus in the vocabulary of reading pedagogy we have a nominalisation like *reading assessment*, which is generally understood to be a process which teachers perform on pupils, and *reading comprehension*, which is generally understood to be a process which readers perform in relation to texts. By nominalising *assessment* and *comprehension*, tense, modality and agency are lost, making it difficult to question how these processes get worked out in actual situations. We view the tendency within the discourse of reading pedagogy to nominalise certain processes as consistent with a broader tendency in the field of reading to technologise otherwise human activities, to standardise and institutionalise activities which are otherwise diverse, and to bestow a stability and formality on activities which might otherwise seem somewhat exploratory and amateur.

Metaphors. Metaphor is a means of representing one aspect of experience in terms of another. We were struck, as we began to compile the list of key words, at the way in which the teaching of reading has used metaphors from fields such as medicine (e.g. 'diagnosis'), the military (e.g. 'code', 'word attack') and business and economics (e.g. 'assessment'). We naturally accept that all language is ultimately metaphorical, and moreover that it is impossible to imagine a vocabulary for the teaching of reading which was not remarkable for its use of metaphors, given the central place held by the teaching of reading in schooling and society. Nevertheless, our view is that the metaphors in the dominant discourse of reading pedagogy are neither accidental nor arbitrary.

Indeed, the significant feature of the metaphors which predominate in the teaching of reading is their consistency: they invoke colder, more mechanistic and more masculine images. They consolidate a connection with the more powerful domains of contemporary social life. It is beyond the scope of this Introduction to attempt to account fully for this phenomenon, as it would require a detailed examination of discourse and social change (and for such an examination see Fairclough, 1992). However, part of the explanation may lie in the concerted efforts made within the reading field, especially during the 1960s and 1970s, to demonstrate its scientific respectability and to establish its status in education, academia and society at large. It achieved this in part by adopting terms which, by their metaphorical associations, explicitly and implicitly forged connections with the more influential and powerful movements of the time.

Patterns of use. One productive way of examining the implicit meanings of terms in the teaching of reading has been to study them in the context of their everyday use (as opposed to studying them in isolation). We have looked for ways in which the terms we have analysed are used – by teachers, by writers and researchers, in official policy documents and by politicians. Sometimes the range of uses in different contexts has been revealing, and sometimes the grammatical constructions typically used in these contexts have provided an insight into implicit meanings.

Specialist and everyday meanings. Another interesting feature of the vocabulary in the teaching of reading is the way that it has invented a number of terms which appear to be highly technical (such as 'phonics' and 'dyslexia'), and at the same time adopted quite ordinary words and infused them with specialist meanings (such as 'functional' and 'readiness'). We have found it helpful when analysing both categories of terms to examine them from points of view other than the one conventionally used within the field of reading, and in particular to see what we could discover about certain terms by examining their meanings outside the teaching of reading. This has helped us to see terms which are very familiar to us, and others in the field, in a new way.

Relational values. As we stated earlier, we were also interested in the way that key terms contained within them implicit ideas about the relationships between people involved in reading events. A number of tools from the field of critical discourse analysis have been helpful here. For example, at the level of vocabulary, we looked for prevalent euphemisms, and the use of markedly formal and informal words, as indicators of social relationships. Where appropriate, we discuss the way that certain terms appear to position teachers and pupils, both in their relationships with each other and in their relationships with others beyond the classroom.

Oppositional quality. We have been struck by the way in which some of these key terms, in some instances or contexts of their use, derive part of their meaning from an implied refutation of an opposing term or concept. This is hardly surprising in a domain of activity as hotly contested as the teaching of reading. We have found support for our approach from a central premise in critical discourse studies: that discourse is the *site* of social struggle, and moreover that discourse is the *stake* in social struggle. For example, we have argued within our entry on 'Readiness' that the meaning of the term cannot be critically understood if it is abstracted from its implied opposition to the terms 'emergent reading' and 'early reading'.

Language and ideology: two caveats

We ought to emphasise at this point that, while our work on this project has been *influenced* by these ideas about language and ideology, it has not been a simple case of applying a contained set of ideas to a list of words and producing a series of entries. For a start, the concepts from discourse analysis and critical language study which we have used were developed for the study of language *in the context of its use,* and not isolated words. Whilst we have tried to relate our analysis of terms to the professional contexts in which we have observed them in use, our analysis nevertheless represents a modified application of discourse analysis.

We should also acknowledge that not all of the entries in the book have been produced by deploying one or more of the practical approaches to language study which we have outlined in this section. Some are much more intuitive and playful than that, and it would be misleading for us to suggest that every entry represented a systematic analysis derived from the tools of critical language study.

The social construction of reading and literacy

In reflecting on the vocabulary of the teaching of reading, we have been influenced by studies that have viewed reading and literacy as socially constructed. These studies have influenced us in two related ways. First, they have emphasised that there is not a single predetermined definition of reading; rather, there are many definitions of reading which emerge from how people actually use written language to interact with each other and to act on the world in which they live. From this perspective, reading and literacy are social and cultural practices and not just a set of decontextualised intellectual skills. This understanding of reading helped us to focus attention on how the vocabulary of the teaching of reading often promotes a single and narrow definition of reading, and it helped us ask questions about the social and cultural dynamics involved in dismissing a broader range of definitions of reading.

A second way in which studies of reading and literacy as socially constructed influenced our investigation was by focusing our attention on the ideological work accomplished by reading. How people engage in reading – how they interact with each other during a reading event, how they interpret a text, how they define what is and what is not reading, and how they connect reading to other events in their lives – reflects a cultural ideology and helps to shape it. Studies of reading as socially constructed give us a warrant for considering reading and the teaching of reading as ideological practices.

In the rest of this section, we briefly discuss reading and literacy as socially constructed, in part to explain why there is no entry in this book for 'Reading' itself. (Readers who are interested in fuller discussions of the social construction of reading may find the following books helpful: *Literacy in theory and practice* by Brian Street; *Cross-cultural approaches to literacy* edited by Brian Street; *Literacy, textbooks and ideology* by Allan Luke; *Literacy as praxis* edited by Catherine Walsh and *The legacies of literacy* by Harvey Graff.)

Reading and literacy have traditionally been viewed as a kind of technology, a technical skill acquired by individuals to be used across situations and texts. Although there might have been some disagreement about which intellectual skills make up reading, there was little disagreement about reading being a set of skills, and that these skills needed to be taught. The view of reading and literacy in general as socially constructed has fundamentally challenged this traditional view of reading. Rather than viewing reading as a decontextualised set of intellectual skills, reading is viewed as a set of social practices and social events involving the use of written language. Researchers studying reading from this perspective ask questions such as: How are people in different situations using written language? What are people using written language for? How do people use written language to interact with each other? What social values are associated with the use of written language? In what ways do people interpret written language? Implicit in these questions is the proposition that the answers will not be generalisable or universal, but specific to a cultural group, a social institution, or perhaps even limited to a particular situation or event. In other words, this view of reading provides a new set of questions to ask about reading and a new definition of knowledge about reading.

Part of the picture that emerges from studies of reading and literacy in specific situations shows that, beyond superficial similarities, there is a great deal of variation in how people use and constitute reading and writing across situations and across cultural groups. For example, in some cultures it is not appropriate to write a letter to express emotion while in others it is the appropriate social practice. In some cultures it is appropriate in particular situations to allow each individual to derive their own interpretation of a written text, while in other cultures in analogous situations the appropriate social practice is to insist on one, single authorised interpretation.

Although there is wide variation in how people engage in reading events, within a social or cultural group people share assumptions about how to engage in reading (including how they should interact with each other) in particular types of situations. For example, members of a church share assumptions about how the prayer book should be read during Sunday services; lawyers share assumptions about how a contract should be read and how it should be disputed; cooks share assumptions about how to use a cookery book; and pupils and teachers share assumptions about how a textbook should be used and read. The wide variation in literacy practices makes it clear that there is not one way of doing reading, but many ways of doing reading, not one literacy but many literacies – and this is true not only across cultural groups but within them as well.

Although it is important to highlight variation, studies of reading as socially constructed have also shown how certain reading practices within an instituion and a society may be associated with the exercise of power. Further, particular reading practices may be associated with greater social prestige and may provide greater access to economic rewards and social mobility. This insight leads to questions such as: Who has access to these reading practices and how do they get access? How is the association between reading practices and the exercise of power rationalised (that is, the ideological justification)? What are the social and cultural consequences of the exercise of power through these reading practices? How is the power which is exercised through these reading practices related to other ways of exercising power? How and to what effect is the exercise of power through these reading practices contested?

We often drew on these ideas about the social construction of reading when writing the entries in this book, by considering the kinds of reading practices which seemed either privileged or marginalised by certain terms, and the kinds of teaching and learning that these terms appeared by implication to authorise or dismiss.

One implication of viewing reading as socially constructed is that the attempt to create a single definition of reading is nonsensical. This is the fundamental disagreement between traditional perspectives on reading and views associated with the social construction of reading. Unless the definition is so superficial as to be of no use (as in 'reading involves written language'), the effect of a single definition of reading is to deny the great variation of social practices that would otherwise count as reading, and would in effect be a description of a specific reading practice rather than a definition of reading *per se*. When a specific reading practice (or a specific set of reading practices) is taken as the definition of reading, other reading practices may be marginalised, or dismissed as not being reading and therefore as not legitimate ways to use written language. *Whoever has the authority to define reading has the power to determine who is a reader and who is not, whose interpretation of a text is acceptable and whose is not, and how and for what written language may be used.* The creation of a single definition of reading (which is itself a literacy practice) creates a standard that legitimates giving power, rewards and resources to those who adhere to authorised reading practices and denies it to others; and, perniciously, it makes the distribution of power based on adherence to a standard model of reading seem common-sensical and unassailable.

Another implication of these studies of reading as socially constructed, for our project on the vocabulary of reading pedagogy, is that is more useful not to define 'Reading' and to leave it vague and indeterminate, than it would be to replace one set of definitions with another. There is, therefore, no entry on 'Reading' in this book.

Procedures for selecting headwords and writing entries

To reiterate, we have unpacked some of the most widely used terms in the teaching of reading, and subjected them to an analysis informed by new approaches to the study of language and ideology, and by new insights into the nature of literacy in society. Our aim has not been to 'demystify' these terms – partly because we do not believe it is a case of discovering their 'true meaning', and partly because there is no evidence to suggest that these terms are widely felt to be mysterious. Quite the contrary: it is their self-evident and taken-for-granted quality which we are trying to fracture.

Our analysis has been organised under twenty-four headwords, each of which will be readily recognised by colleagues working in the field as fairly typical of terms used in the teaching of reading, whose influence is profound and whose underlying meanings, values and assumptions are curiously impervious to examination. Some readers will no doubt wish that we had included words that are missing, or that we had not bothered with some of the entries which are included. We have not attempted to be comprehensive. We hope that readers will be motivated by what we have done here to apply similar methods to other key terms – both in the teaching of reading and elsewhere.

To decide on our headwords, we began by writing down every term we could think of which was used in a technical or professional capacity in the field. This produced a list of over 100 words. We then grouped the words into clusters of words with linked meanings or uses. Some words were assigned to more than one cluster.

This produced about thirty clusters. At this stage we attempted to identify which word in each cluster represented what we called the 'superordinate' term. We did this by discussing the way the words in each cluster were used in the field, and the kinds of relationships they seemed to have with each other. These twenty-five or so headwords then served as our agenda for writing entries, and remained fairly stable throughout the writing. In the final editing stages, some entries were combined, producing the final list.

Some entries seemed more appropriately handled in a relatively serious and academic register; others seemed more effectively approached light-heartedly or irreverently (but not, we hope, mean-spiritedly). And, as we have said earlier, some entries reflect our attempt to apply the concepts and analytical tools from studies of language and literacy, while other entries are more intuitive, or experimental, or playful. The entries were not produced by merely applying a standard set of procedures to each key term: the process was more exploratory, reflective and varied than that, and we tried as far as possible to approach each entry in a way which seemed fitting and faithful to the term in question. As we discussed each entry, we were able to use our different backgrounds (in particular the differences in perspective between the UK and the US) to enrich what we wrote.

It is, of course, inevitable that some of what we've written in the entries will reflect our own professional 'positions' within various debates on the teaching of reading. Indeed, to be consistent with the principles informing the book we would have to say that *any* commentary on aspects of the teaching of reading will be informed by values, assumptions and allegiances. We have tried to pitch the entries at the level of critical analysis, on the assumption that this is not only more appropriate for a project of this kind but also more likely to avoid some of the more acrimonious pockets of in-fighting in this field. We have not tried to conceal our own positions, and are sure that we have not done so. However, we have decided that it would be inappropiate for us to try to set out those positions explicitly here, since these have been made clear in other of our writings.

We have organised our commentary under twenty-four headwords presented in alphabetical order. However, the reader should not feel obliged to read the entries in sequence, since they have only been organised this way for ease of use. Do plot your own route through the entries; no 'reading' of the book is the preferred reading. However, we would discourage readers from using the book as a conventional reference book, in which words are 'looked up' and treated in isolation from each other. Our hope is that the book as a whole achieves more than the sum of its individual entries, and that readers will approach the book as a whole, irrespective of the order in which they read the entries.

Implications for research and practice

It has been our aim in this project to contribute to the work of professionals working in schools, in teacher education and in research, though this contribution will naturally be more in the way of inviting a particular kind of reflection on the issues we have raised than of providing ideas which may be directly translated into practice. We have also tried to make a small contribution to the two theoretical perspectives which have informed our work. With respect to the field of critical discourse analysis, we have applied a conceptual framework and a practical method, which were devised for the analysis of texts (spoken, written and visual), to an influential professional vocabulary made up of discrete words. By adapting the insights of critical discourse analysis to the study of this fairly stylised vocabulary we have been able to look across the individual words for patterns of meaning which were not previously accessible. With respect to studies of the social construction of reading, we have through our entries provided an analysis of one of the ways in which the tension between a single dominant definition of reading, and a view of reading as socially constructed, gets played out in a pivotal professional context.

We began this Introduction by recalling our own personal encounters with the vocabulary of reading pedagogy as novice teachers. We can now see that one function of this discourse is to acculturate new recruits to the teaching profession into its distinctive values and assumptions, and to make into common sense what is neither common nor necessarily sensible or sensitive. The analysis in this book might therefore serve to sensitise colleagues involved in teacher education to the power of this discourse. We hope that they will encourage students intending to be teachers to apply this kind of critical analysis to key terms in order to sharpen their awareness of its significance, influence and consequences.

We do not believe that changing terminology, in and of itself, changes attitudes and practice. However, we hope that this analysis will raise the awareness of practitioners and sensitise them to the messages which their specialist vocabulary implicitly conveys, and the power of that vocabulary to influence understanding, marginalise certain groups, exclude certain ideas and practices, and oversimplify complex processes. In this sense our project's overarching aim has been to provide some tools for questioning the common-sense quality of the vocabulary in the teaching of reading, and in the process sharpen classroom practice for the benefit of pupils.

Bibliography

On language and ideology

Bakhtin, Mikhail (ed. Holquist, M.) (1981) *The dialogic imagination: four essays.* Austin: University of Texas Press

Clark, Romy; Fairclough, Norman; Ivanič, Ros and Martin-Jones, Marilyn (1988) *Critical language awareness.* Lancaster: Centre for Language in Social Life Research Papers 1, University of Lancaster

Eagleton, Terry (1991) *Ideology: an introduction.* London: Verso

Fairclough, Norman (1989) *Language and power.* London: Longman

Fairclough, Norman (1992) *Discourse and social change.* Cambridge: Polity Press

Foucault, Michel (1977) *The archaeology of knowledge.* London: Tavistock

Goffman, Erving (1974) *Frame analysis.* New York: Harper Colophon Books

Hall, Stuart (1982) 'The rediscovery of "ideology": return to the repressed in media studies' in Gurevitch, M. *et al.* (eds) *Culture, society and the media.* London: Methuen

Halliday, Michael A.K. (1978) *Language as social semiotic: the social interpretation of language and meaning.* London: Edward Arnold

Kristeva, Julia (1970) *Le texte du roman.* The Hague: Mouton

Volosinov, V.I. (1929, trans. 1973) *Marxism and the philosophy of language.* London: Seminar Press

Williams, Raymond (1976) *Keywords: a vocabulary of culture and society.* London: Fontana

Williams, Raymond (1977) *Marxism and literature.* Oxford: Oxford University Press

On the social construction of reading and literacy

Barton, David (1994) *Literacy: an introduction to the ecology of written language.* Oxford: Blackwell

Barton, David and Ivanič, Roz (eds) (1991) *Writing in the community.* London: Sage

Brodkey, Linda (1987) *Academic writing as social practice.* Philadelphia: Temple University Press

Cook-Gumperz, Jenny (ed.) (1986) *The social construction of literacy.* Cambridge: Cambridge University Press

Graff, Harvey (1987) *The legacies of literacy: continuities and contradictions in western culture and society.* Bloomington: University of Indiana Press

Luke, Allan (1988) *Literacy, textbooks and ideology.* Barcombe: The Falmer Press

Maybin, Janet (ed.) (1994) *Language and literacy in social practice.* Clevedon: Multilingual Matters

Schieffelin, Bambi and Gilmore, Perry (eds) (1986) *The acquisition of literacy: ethnographic perspectives.* Norwood, NJ: Ablex Publishing Corporation

Street, Brian (1984) *Literacy in theory and practice.* Cambridge: Cambridge University Press.

Street, Brian (ed.) (1993) *Cross-cultural approaches to literacy.* Cambridge: Cambridge University Press

Walsh, Catherine (ed.) (1991) *Literacy as praxis: culture, language and pedagogy.* Norwood, NJ: Ablex Publishing Corporation

Willinsky, John (1990) *The new literacy: redefining reading and writing in the schools.* New York: Routledge

THE ENTRIES

Ability (Reading ability)

> There is much conjecture about the reading ability of 7 year olds today as compared to that in previous years.
>
> A language for life *(The Bullock Report, 1975), p. 23*

Reading ability is a term that is very often used in the teaching of reading – so often, in fact, that its meaning appears to be self-evident and its underlying assumptions and values appear to be neutral. **Reading ability** is widely understood to mean *how well someone reads*. We may disagree about how a person's **reading ability** has been judged, but the term itself has a persistently unproblematical quality to it.

However, **reading ability** may be more complex and less neutral than it first appears to be. We can see this by looking at the term in three different ways. First, it's worth thinking about the everyday contexts in which the term **reading ability** is used. It's always used in connection with an evaluative judgement being made about an individual or a group, in comparison with another individual or group, or when discussing standards or trends over time. The quotation from the Bullock Report at the top of this page is a typical example. In fact, this term is more often used in relation to groups (or 'cohorts' or even 'populations') than to individuals, which illustrates the point we're making here. There is generally an air of earnest concern surrounding its use. The contexts in which the term is typically used therefore give it a loading which links it to judgements, comparisons and concern.

Second, there is an in-built ambiguity in the term **reading ability**, since we use the term's root, 'able', in two distinctly different ways. We use 'able' to mean native talent (as in 'the able child'), and we use it to mean acquired skill (as in 'finally able to ride a bike'). So in this sense it's not entirely clear whether **reading ability** refers to a person's potential to learn to read (that is, their ability to benefit from teaching) or to their actual level of reading. Granted, few people really believe that children become readers solely on the strength of their native talent. However, the ambiguity inherent in the term **reading ability** helps to explain why quantifiable measures of **reading ability**, like 'reading age' for example (see separate entry), are often used within the education system as substitutes for 'intelligence', following the discrediting of IQ as a valid index of mental potential in the 1970s. In this sense, **reading ability** has a rather different meaning from 'able to read'.

This ambiguity raises a further question. Does **reading ability** relate to a person's actual *performance* in reading, or to a more abstract *competence* which may or may not be realised in practice? Both of these could be described as forms of **reading ability**, and often are. More often, though, the term **reading ability** is used to stand for the competence rather than to the performance. It seems possible, for example, to say that a child's **reading ability** (i.e. competence) is good, but that their performance is poor (i.e. what they choose to read, how often they read, the quality of their oral reading, their attitude to reading, their degree of understanding and involvement, etc.). This kind of distinction is often applied to kids who 'can read but don't'. Here, **reading ability** sometimes becomes a way of explaining differences between children whose overt reading behaviour is very similar (and usually disappointing) but whose underlying competence is considered to be different. In this sense, the meaning of **reading ability** comes close to 'able to read', but differs from 'does a lot of good reading'.

Let's look at this idea from a slightly different angle. Individuals may (regrettably?) perform below their level of **reading ability**, but no one could possibly be expected to achieve beyond their level of **reading ability**. This common-sense view assumes that reading is located within individuals, and that it is a possession owned by individual readers. **Reading ability** is a fixed and finite resource, a commodity which is unequally distributed in the population – not because of different teaching approaches, or disparities in resourcing, or even necessarily social background. In this way the term itself reflects, and at the same time helps to perpetuate, the essentially liberal and meritocratic idea that differences between people in their reading achievement represent a rational stratification based on their **reading ability**.

Finally, there is a further meaning which we associate with the term **ability**. In addition to meaning 'can', *able* also means 'may' – that is, to be allowed to do, to have permission to do. There is therefore an implication that those with **reading ability** have been allowed to read or to learn to read, or at least have been given permission to read certain things, at certain times, or in certain ways. It's possible then to perceive, in the difference between those with high and low **reading ability**, an element of selection and exclusion – not just a difference between the haves and the have-nots, but also between the *mays* and the *may-nots*. When the young pupil says that she 'isn't able to read this book', this ambiguity is sharply focused: does she feel that the book is too difficult for her, that it is beyond her current level of competence; or is she saying that someone in authority (possibly a teacher) has not given her permission to read it, either by expressly prohibiting her from reading it, or by doing so in more subtle ways?

Accuracy (Accuracy in reading)

Ironically enough, it's exceedingly difficult to pin the term **accuracy** down with any precision. How accurate does one's reading have to be for it to be considered accurate? Who decides? Is **accuracy** a continuum, with some readings being more or less accurate than other readings, or is it an all-or-nothing, with some readings being accurate and other readings being inaccurate? What kind of reading does **accuracy** refer to? Does it refer to the rendering of written language into spoken language – that is, to the **accuracy** of an oral rendering of a text? Or does it refer to comprehending the meaning of a text – that is, to the **accuracy** of one's understanding?

Despite these uncertainties, there is no doubt that **accuracy** holds a powerful position in the discourse of reading pedagogy. This is partly because an emphasis upon **accuracy** in reading is consistent with the importance placed on precision elsewhere in the teaching of reading and in education generally. Perhaps we should add that this is consistent with a wider obsession with **accuracy** and precision in our culture. Nevertheless, within the teaching of reading the term **accuracy** encapsulates common-sense understandings about the goals of reading and learning to read.

At the level of rendering written language into spoken language, the term **accuracy** is generally used to mean a perfect match between the graphic symbols on the page and the spoken rendering of those symbols. This sense of **accuracy** makes several assumptions:

- that **accuracy** at this level can only be demonstrated in a spoken rendering – that is, it requires a set of practices which enable the text to be rendered into spoken language;

- that print is essentially speech written down, and that 'reading' involves the recovery of the original spoken form (see **Code**);

- that 'errors' at this level are a symptom of deficient or undeveloped proficiency, rather than part of a productive and worthwhile process;

- that an 'accurate' spoken rendering of a text is both important for its own sake and an essential precondition for understanding.

We can take this sense of **accuracy** a step further and recognise that one implication of the term **accuracy** is that a spoken rendering of a text is only truly accurate when it is rendered in the dialect denoted by the graphic symbols or in the dialect intended by the author. In this sense some spoken renderings of a text might be considered inaccurate if they are spoken in certain accents, or with certain intonation patterns, or with certain letters treated as silent and/or vocalised.

At the level of comprehending the meaning of a text, the term **accuracy** is generally taken to mean a perfect match between the reader's understanding of a text's meaning and the author's intended meaning – or, more typically, the meaning which a text is conventionally taken to have (its 'authorised' meaning within certain groups and institutions). Here again, a number of assumptions are made:

- that all texts have a single meaning (which is either self-evident or attainable through careful study, irrespective of context, purpose, etc.); and

- that locating the text's 'true' meaning is the essential purpose of reading it.

The implications of the term **accuracy**, when these two levels of reading are taken together, suggest that there is little difference between the common-sense meaning of '**accuracy** in reading' and the common-sense meaning of 'reading' itself. To read something is to read it accurately. Anything else isn't reading: it's either guessing, or misunderstanding, or both.

Of course, not all reading pedagogies subscribe to an overriding emphasis on a narrow definition of **accuracy**. In some pedagogies, oral reading 'errors' are not only tolerated but are seen as productive, in that they show that the reader is making efforts to gain meaning from a text and provide the teacher with insights into those efforts. Also, some pedagogies adopt a broader definition of comprehension, so that understanding can be demonstrated not through trivial answers to superficial comprehension questions but through personal responses, multiple interpretations and so on. However, we would argue that these pedagogies have merely broadened the definition of **accuracy** that underpins classroom practices rather than challenged the fundamental notion of **accuracy** which we are trying to identify here. For example, within those pedagogies which view oral reading errors as productive, errors are still errors, even though they may be called something else: they are simply re-cast as productive errors. Outside the range of errors which are treated as productive errors, there will almost certainly be errors which are nothing more than errors. And within those pedagogies which adopt a broader definition of comprehension, there will still be readings outside the range of acceptable readings which will still be seen as nothing more than symptoms of a lack of understanding. Within these newer pedagogies, most of the assumptions highlighted in the third and fourth paragraphs of this entry are left pretty much intact. Certainly, pupils will approach tasks within these newer pedagogies with the firm belief that there is a notion of **accuracy** informing them, however adept they are at discerning that notion and accommodating to it. This underlying current of **accuracy**, in an apparently shifting tide of pedagogical practice, is almost inescapable within our system of schooling as it is currently structured, which takes us back to our original point about the meaning of the term **accuracy** in reading being located in a broader discourse of precision in education and society.

To determine whether you have read this entry accurately, answer the following questions:

1.   How accurate does one's reading have to be for it to be considered accurate?

2.   Who decides?

3.   Is **accuracy** a continuum, with some readings being more or less accurate than other readings, or is it an all-or-nothing, with some readings being accurate and other readings being inaccurate?

4.   What kind of reading does **accuracy** refer to? Does it refer to the rendering of written language into spoken language – that is, to the **accuracy** of an oral rendering of a text? Or does it refer to comprehending the meaning of a text – that is, to the **accuracy** of one's understanding?

5.   Who is authorised to ask these questions?

6.   Who is authorised to judge whether your answers to these questions reflect an *accurate* reading? Are you?

Our point in asking these questions is to illustrate that any conception of **accuracy** in the teaching of reading will be based on unequal power relations between the reader and the arbiter of **accuracy**, and that the existence of unequal power relations between readers and arbiters makes some notion of **accuracy** inevitable.

Assessment (Reading assessment)

Like several other terms in the discourse of reading pedagogy, the term **reading assessment** is something of a misnomer, in that the meaning suggested by the combination of **reading** and **assessment** is not at all the meaning normally denoted by the composite term. The term does not really refer to an estimation or evaluation of reading, or of a reading. The activity in question does not generally involve a judgement about a specific oral rendering of a text, or an account of a text's meaning, or of a particular response to a text, in a way which is separate from the person doing the reading. A more apt and descriptive term might therefore be 'reader assessment', since it is ultimately something about the reader which is being evaluated.

> **Assessment**
>
> 1. The determination or adjustment of the amount of taxation, charge, fine, etc., to be paid by a person or community.
>
> 2. The scheme of charge or taxation so adjusted.
>
> 3. The amount of charge so determined upon.
>
> 4. Official valuation of property or income for the purposes of taxation; the value assigned to it.
>
> 5. *fig.* in gen. sense: Estimation, evaluation.
>
> *from* The Compact Edition of the Oxford English Dictionary
> *Oxford University Press, 1971*

We detect in the term **reading assessment** a fundamental tension between two conceptions of **reading assessment**, which might be characterised as *reading assessment as science* and *reading assessment as art*. The conception of *reading assessment as science* calls to mind precision instruments and technical procedures which do their work independently of human judgement. These instruments (such as tests, for example) are assumed to be neutral with respect to different competing definitions of reading, even though particular notions about reading inevitably inform their construction. These instruments are also assumed to be neutral with respect to the ways in which their results are interpreted and used. That is, any 'misuse' of the results of *reading assessment as science* cannot be blamed on the technology, since the technology is strictly disinterested (see **Reading age**).

The conception of *reading assessment as art* instead draws upon the everyday classroom reality of **reading assessment**. This everyday experience suggests that

reading assessment is a complex judgement-making process mediated through social relationships and patterns of interaction. Within this conception, it is the teacher, working within an elaborate professional and institutional setting, who is in effect the 'instrument' for assessing reading. And within this conception, even the interpretation and use of the results produced by the 'instruments' of *reading assessment as science* are socially-embedded processes – let alone the more routine judgements which teachers make about children's competence as readers.

This tension is expressed through two of the comments most frequently made by teachers about **reading assessment**: 'We are assessing all the time' (implying the notion of *reading assessment as art*), and 'We aren't very accurate or consistent in our assessments' (implying the notion of *reading assessment as science*).

It is interesting to note that, of all the domains in the teaching of reading, it is in the domain of making judgements about readers' competence that some of the most interesting metaphors have been adopted. In addition to **assessment**, we have diagnosis, evaluation, standards (see **Standards**), scores, norms, discrimination, monitoring, reliability, validity and screening, to name a few. 'Diagnosis' is a good example of the tendency within the discourse of reading pedagogy to import terms from the world of medicine and medical pathology. It calls to mind people in white coats working in clean laboratories, clinical and precise. It suggests a dispassionate description of presenting symptoms, free of personal values or judgements, and neutral with respect to either causes on the one hand or suitable treatment on the other. The ideological work done by the term *diagnosis* is therefore to divest the process, of judging a reader's competence, of the subjectivity which is an essential and inevitable element of it. The term also serves to align the process with the world of medical science, with its laws and methods.

'Evaluation', in contrast, has been imported into the teaching of reading vocabulary (and educational discourse generally) from the market-place. It explicitly involves an assignment of value, but not the exercise of 'values' as in 'personal beliefs and priorities'. Evaluation shares with diagnosis an implied neutrality with respect to cause and treatment, and an independence from human judgement. Evaluation calls to mind the exactitude of weighing scales and the ability to distinguish between fine differences of monetary value. There is also a suggestion of exchanging one commodity for another, or one currency with another, of determining the equivalence of one thing in the terms of another. The implication for reading is that evaluation involves the precise conversion of a reader's competence into a different scale of value. The ideological work done by the term *evaluation* is therefore to neutralise the process of judging a reader's competence, but also to align the process with the world of economics, with its models and regulations, its rewards and penalties, its credits and debits, its rebates and taxes.

Portfolio **assessment** can be associated with the discourse of art, or with the discourse of stocks, bonds and investment. Portfolio **assessment** defies the easy translation of reading artefacts into scores, although there have been attempts to do so. Yet, whether associated with art or economic investment, portfolios are sites of valuation, determinations of worth translated into judgements of achievement and educability.

This proliferation of mechanistic, pseudo-scientific and economic metaphors in the dominant discourse of reading pedagogy serves in part to position teachers as rather feeble novices who should really leave the heavy stuff to the experts. It's little wonder that the professional backlash has adopted a warm and nurturing language, with lots of 'listening in to the child becoming a reader'. To date, the backlash has eschewed nominalisation; just lots of affirming process words. Yet despite whatever allegiance one might feel towards a warm and nurturing language, and despite whatever relief one might feel about the supplanting of mechanistic metaphors with processes, questions still need to be asked about what ideological work this alternative discourse does, apart from declaring an opposition.

Bedtime story reading

Bedtime story reading elicits warm feelings and images of mothers cuddling with their young children around a favourite story book. Perhaps they are reading a fairy tale as the child drifts off to sleep. It is an intimate moment, evoking powerful and positive emotions and memories for some people, perhaps for many.

One way to view **bedtime story reading** is as a family practice, a time for parents and children to be together, enjoying a story and each other – provided, of course, that they do indeed enjoy the activity. Reading one story to one child is not the same as having to read many stories to several children, each arguing over which story is to be read and having to do so night after night. It is not always an enjoyable activity after a hard day of work, and for single parents it can be extra burdensome. The image of **bedtime story reading** is an idealised one, not at all consistent with the variety and complexity of emotions involved in the reality of everyday life. It is important to note that the dominant image of **bedtime story reading** is typically of a *mother* and child, which of course may not always be realised in practice but is persistent nevertheless.

Bedtime story reading undoubtedly originated as a family-based activity. However, more recently several *educational* claims have been made for **bedtime story reading**. It is claimed that **bedtime story reading** prepares the child for learning to read in school; it gives the child book knowledge, story knowledge and print awareness; it teaches the child the discourse of school instruction; it gives young children an interest in and motivation for reading; and it may even teach some children to read before they get to school, among other benefits. Children who have a long history of **bedtime story reading** before they entered school are claimed to do better in school and learn to read faster. Such claims have led some teachers and politicians to promote **bedtime story reading,** and to teach mothers how to do **bedtime story reading** as part of encouraging them to be good parents.

This suggests a second way of viewing **bedtime story reading**: as an educational activity and not merely as a family activity. From this point of view, parents – and in most cases mothers – who do *not* do **bedtime story reading** may not be providing their children with the experiences that they may need for learning to read. Especially targeted by educationists and politicians are parents who may themselves have difficulties with reading. Typical of this educational view are two articles that appeared in *The Observer* (6 June 1993, pp. 13 and 22, respectively) with the headlines, 'Blitz on illiteracy to be launched from mother's knee' and 'Educate the parents, save the child'. In the first, an American 'expert' was invited to Whitehall to brief ministers, and was quoted as saying: 'By teaching the parents, you get a double-dollar effect [*sic*]. You are improving the child's scores at school and the mother's life at home and work.' The second article makes bolder claims: '...based on extensive research, across three continents, showing that *regardless of social class* children who receive parental support and help, especially in the early years, do better educationally, are much less likely to be involved in crime, are emotionally more stable, and lead happier lives. And they are much less likely to become a single parent.'

Needless to say, it would be essential to evaluate the research evidence on which these extravagant claims are allegedly based before drawing conclusions about their validity. The claims made for **bedtime story reading** imply that the reason parents do not help their children is either that they do not know how to do so (they are ignorant parents), or that they do not want to do so (they are feckless parents). It is important to note that the reference to 'parents' in the reports and newspaper articles is to 'mothers' and not to fathers, regardless of whether they say so explicitly. It is yet another version of blaming mothers for social and educational problems, implying an erosion of family values and of the family itself.

Almost all parents want to help their children learn to read and to do well in school. Many parents who do not know how to read well will take adult literacy classes after their children are born just to be able to help them. Others will make arrangements for other relatives or friends to be available to help their children. What prevents parents from helping their children as much as they would like is often not unwillingness or lack of knowledge, but the economic and social constraints of daily life. While the constraints may not be as severe for middle-class mothers as for working-class mothers, the constraints are nonetheless real for them as well. Almost all parents welcome knowledge that may be helpful to their children's growth and education. But to assert that the problem is that parents – mothers – need training, in parenting and in **bedtime story reading**, is tantamount to asserting that women ought to stay home more with their children and be out in the world of work less. It is to suggest that the difficulties that some pupils have with learning to read are not due to inappropriate teaching, or underfunding and understaffing of schools, or lack of child care, but rather to the failure of mothers to stay home and look after their children and family, with **bedtime story reading** being part of the image.

Part of what is noteworthy about **bedtime story reading** is its transformation from a family activity to an educational activity. As a family activity its primary purpose was for the enjoyment and intimacy of parents and children. There was no need to push the activity onto parents or to teach them how to do it (properly). Indeed, there was no right or wrong way to do it. When **bedtime story reading** becomes/became an educational activity, however benignly it is adopted and then promoted by schools, enjoyment and intimacy become secondary concerns. Enjoyment and intimacy become only means to an end (educational and social achievement), rather than ends in themselves. By transforming **bedtime story reading** into an educational activity, schools and government institutions encroach further into the family, and locate a cause of social and educational decline in the 'inadequacies' of mothers.

Code

Definition 1: Cracking the code

Reading is occasionally described as 'cracking the **code**', as if print were a secret **code** used by spies and the reader is a detective unravelling a mystery in order to get at a hidden message. A secret **code** cannot be secret from everyone. There must be an 'in' group who know the secret **code**, and an 'out' group from whom the message is being hidden. One of the functions of a secret **code** is to make clear who is in the 'in' group and who is not.

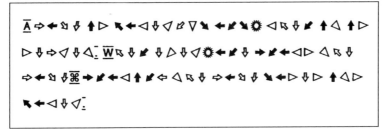

Translation appears at the end of this entry

Anthropologists who have studied secret societies and organisations often find that the effort put into keeping what the group does secret is not necessarily justified by what the group's activities are. It is often the secrecy and mystery itself which gives the group power, not necessarily what the group actually does.

Breaking the **code** in reading typically means translating written symbols into spoken language. It implies that spoken language is primary and meaningful and that written language is a camouflage of spoken language. It is interesting that spoken language is rarely described as a **code**, although spoken words are no less symbols that written words. An assumption is made that meaning is readily available and obvious in spoken language. The task for readers is to break the written language **code** down into spoken language, and thus **code**-breaking highlights phonics and other word-attack systems that teach how the **code** can be broken down into spoken language eschewing meaning. Defining reading as **code**-breaking emphasises accuracy, as in accurately translating the written **code** into spoken language (see **Accuracy in reading**).

The metaphor of reading as **code**-breaking also suggests qualities about the successful reader. She/he is clever (to have cracked the **code**) and diligent (because cracking the **code** requires hard work and persistence). Children who learn early how to crack the **code** are viewed as especially clever. Those who fail to crack the **code** lack those qualities.

The strange symbols of a **code**, like the ones above, can be intimidating. But written language is not a strange **code**. Children are surrounded with print and play with print from an early age. It is not a strange task to connect meaning to the symbols. In order for print to be a **code**, the symbols must be made strange. We have made the symbols of print strange in the example above by changing the graphic form of the symbols. But there are other ways to make written language strange.

E4	C5
D3	G6
NC3	BG7
NF3	D6
BE2	NF6
0-0	0-0

The symbols in the **code** directly above are familiar letters and numbers. What makes the **code** strange – at least strange to many – is that readers may not know where to 'locate' the **code**. By knowing that the **code** refers to the beginning of a game of chess, the **code** becomes less strange. Cracking the **code** by transforming the written symbols into spoken language helps little in understanding the message. In order to understand the message you need to know how the game of chess is played and what information is assumed in recording chess games (the left-hand column is white, the right is black, the chess board is lettered and numbered in a particular way, and no symbol is given for pawns). Moreover, some chess players will recognise the use of a particular chess opening and a particular defence and especially experienced readers will recognise that both white and black made errors in their openings that the other failed to take advantage of. Readers who know the functions of recording chess games – to have a record of what occurred in case the board is tipped over, to review the game to learn from mistakes, and to have the game printed in a chess magazine if the game is especially important or unusual – may predict that both chess players will be unhappy with themselves later for missing an opportunity to take advantage of their opponent's mistake.

Cracking the **code** of a chess game is not a matter of transforming written symbols into spoken language but of making the print meaningful. Making the print meaningful requires an understanding of where the print is 'located' (a chess game)and how that genre or type of print is used in that 'location', as well as knowledge about the topic and an interest in the meaning of the print. The assumptions implied in defining reading as cracking the **code** do not include understanding 'location', readers' knowledge of language or of the world, or the interests and agendas of readers.

We suspect that many readers will not make the effort to crack the **code** in the first example above but will instead skip to the note at the end of this entry. That they chose not to crack the **code** does not mean that they are less clever than those who do and it does not mean that they are less diligent; yet such judgements are promoted by defining reading as cracking the **code**. Further, we suspect that some readers will wonder why the passages above were written in a strange **code** when they could have been presented as ordinary and familiar language – which is a good question to ask about reading pedagogies that treat written language as a strange **code**.

Definition 2: Code as manners
In some restaurants, a sign is posted stating the establishment's dress **code,** e.g. 'jacket and tie required'. In some clubs, and in various professions, a **code** of behaviour is required – a set of manners expected of members. Similarly, it often seems as if there is a **code** of behaviour, a set of manners, for members of the 'reading club'. Readers are expected to behave appropriately with print; to have a mannered reading. While the **code** of behaviour varies depending on the situation, often the **code** of behaviour for classroom reading includes reading what one is given to read, when, where, and how one is told to do so; interpreting print in a manner consistent with the expectations of others; and handling print in a respectful manner (e.g. not tearing out pages, not marking-up books, not writing on others' papers). To not follow the **code** is to put oneself and perhaps one's family at risk of being viewed as morally inadequate. To the extent that following the **code** and becoming a member of the classroom reading 'club' is associated with individual qualities (e.g. being clever, of good moral character, hard-working), members can assume intellectual and moral superiority over those who are not members. To the extent that the **code** of behaviour required by the club is justified as a better way to behave, the way of life of those in the club is viewed as superior to those outside it and the benefits acquired by club members justified on the basis of a superior way of life.

Translation of coded message on p.27
A code is powerful only when it is secret. When everyone knows the code, knowing the code loses its power.

Comprehension

The term **comprehension** is so utterly familiar to anyone who has worked in the reading area that there seems very little to say about it other than that it is a synonym for 'understanding what is read'. We can argue about the nature of **comprehension**, how it is learned, and how it should be taught and assessed, but as a key term in the teaching of reading it seems straightforward enough. However, the first thing that struck us when we tried to stand back from this term and look at it afresh was that it seems an unnecessarily technical word for something as fundamental as 'understanding what is read'. Why adopt a fancy word like **comprehension** in the first place? Why not 'understanding'? It is true that we have slogans within the teaching of reading such as 'reading with understanding', but with the existence of the superordinate term **comprehension**, the slogan 'reading with understanding' has a folksy, vernacular feel to it.

The term **comprehension**, like a number of terms in the teaching of reading, has its roots in the academic discipline of psychology, which assumed a proprietorial interest in reading in the early years of this century. Psychologists applied technical terms (usually nominalisations) to aspects of human thought and behaviour in order to distinguish the scientific study of them from their 'lay' meanings. 'Thinking' became 'cognition'; 'feeling' became 'affect'; and 'understanding' became **comprehension**. **Comprehension** is therefore an example of the tendency in the field of reading, which we identified in the Introduction, to technologise otherwise 'ordinary' human activities.

To understand **comprehension** it is helpful to view the term historically, in particular the development of its prominence in opposition to the heavy emphasis on oral rendition and oral fluency that was widespread until the 1960s.

The teaching of reading in the United Kingdom and the United States has historically emphasised oral reading, not **comprehension**. The McGuffy readers, which were popular from the mid-1800s until the early 1900s, consisted of a series of passages arranged in increasing difficulty to be read orally and practised for fluency. Children read the passages aloud either in a group or individually, monitored and corrected by their teachers. The basal readers and reading schemes of the 1940s, 1950s, 1960s, and even many basal reading programmes and reading schemes in the 1970s, were based on the same conception of reading education as the McGuffy readers – the practice of oral reading on increasingly difficult passages.

Similarly, the history of reading research shows that the equation of reading with **comprehension** is a recent phenomenon. Although early reading researchers such as Edmund Huey, whose book on reading was published in 1908 (Huey, 1908), had written about **comprehension**, it was their experiments on perception and oral reading that became important. Before Huey, empirical research on reading was virtually non-existent. There were essays and opinions about the nature of reading supported by limited experience and observation, if supported at all. Huey, who began conducting experiments on reading about the same time as psychology was becoming a recognised discipline, systematised research on reading by using empirical scientific methods. The result was an experimental emphasis on observable behaviour, namely oral reading. Subsequent reading researchers built on the work of Huey and his contemporaries by continuing to emphasise the psychology of reading, empirical experiments, observable behaviour, perception and oral reading.

The emphasis on oral reading continued in reading research and in reading education until the 1960s with the emergence of cognitive psychology, modern linguistics and psycholinguistics. (Although the roots of cognitive psychology and linguistics can be traced back earlier than the 1960s, their influence on the field of reading research and reading education did not become prominent and widespread until the 1960s.) These disciplines shifted the emphasis from observable behaviour to what might be going on in the mind. Instead of emphasising oral reading, **comprehension** was emphasised.

The new emphasis on **comprehension** was reflected in reading tests, basal reading programmes and reading schemes, although there were many battles between educators who wanted to emphasise oral reading and those who wanted to emphasise **comprehension**. Such battles were perhaps most fierce around early reading instruction and the instruction provided to older pupils who had difficulty with reading. Some advocated a firm and solid grounding in oral reading while others argued for a grounding in **comprehension**.

But what was **comprehension**? For most reading educators and researchers, the definition of **comprehension** was taken for granted. **Comprehension** was understanding the meaning in the text. The better a pupil could understand the meaning of the text, and the meaning of more difficult texts, the better the reader. Reading tests reflected this simplistic definition of **comprehension**. Pupils read a passage and answered questions which had predetermined right and wrong answers. Similarly, reading education programmes emphasised getting the right answer to questions about the meaning of what pupils were told to read.

On some reading tests, the level of **comprehension** was divided into levels by grade. Based on readability formulae, the passages pupils read were divided into reading grade levels. By answering the **comprehension** questions correctly a pupil was able to show that she/he was able to read at that reading grade level. While the specific percentages varied, in general pupils who were able to answer 90 per cent of the **comprehension** questions correctly at a particular reading grade level were deemed to be reading at an independent level at that reading grade level (they did not need the teacher's help in reading passages at that grade level); above 80 per cent correct was the instructional level (they needed the teacher's help); and below 80 per cent was the frustration level (even with the teacher's help they were not able to read a passage at this grade level). The selection of the percentages used to determine independent, instructional and frustration levels seems to have been arbitrary but, with slight variation, widespread.

Early on, reading researchers and reading educators realised that there was a difference between answering a **comprehension** question that was overtly noted in the passage and answering a **comprehension** question that required 'reading between the lines'. Distinctions were made between literal **comprehension** and inferential **comprehension**. Further types of **comprehension** were added – critical **comprehension**, application, appreciation, character development, linear **comprehension**, global **comprehension**, sequential **comprehension**, cause and effect **comprehension**, among many others – and reading education programmes and reading researchers often differed on how many different types of **comprehension** there were and how they should be labelled.

Research on **comprehension** showed that how much pupils understood of what they read, and what they understood, varied depending on the knowledge they already had. Further, other factors such as where the pupils were, or what subject they were in (English or art), also influenced how much and what they comprehended. For some reading researchers and reading educators, these findings meant that pupils should be given the needed background knowledge and appropriate context so that they could correctly comprehend the text they were assigned to read. This view was based on the notion that a passage or text had a true meaning, that it was the reader's task to get the true meaning out of the text, and that it was the teacher's task to help the reader do so. Learning to comprehend – learning to read – was learning how to get the true meaning out of the text.

However, other reading researchers and reading educators argued that the influence of background knowledge and context on **comprehension** required a fundamental shift in the definition of **comprehension**. Rather than viewing meaning as located in the text, and rather than there being one true meaning, these reading researchers and reading educators viewed **comprehension** as an interaction (sometimes called a transaction) between the reader and the text. The meanings, knowledge and information in the text interacted with the meanings, knowledge and information the reader already had, yielding new meaning, knowledge and information. **Comprehension** could vary from reader to reader and from one situation to another.

The view of **comprehension** as differing across readers caused many reading educators to rethink how they taught reading, how they evaluated progress in learning to read and how they organised their classrooms. Other reading educators and reading researchers found the variability in **comprehension** too messy and at odds with their belief that texts had a true meaning or, if not a true meaning, a conventional meaning that pupils were expected to be able to derive. Although both groups of reading educators may agree that background knowledge and context affect **comprehension**, their views on the implications of that for defining **comprehension** and for reading education are very different, incompatible and often antagonistic.

Recently, the centrality of **comprehension** for reading research and reading education has waned as the field has become increasingly multidisciplinary. The influence of anthropology, for example, has emphasised that there are different ways of reading and that reading needs to be viewed as part of cultural activities. Rather than view pupils' background culture as influencing their **comprehension**, **comprehension** in school is itself viewed as a cultural activity and not just a psychological process. Literary theories have raised questions about the location of meaning as being in a text, a reader, or between them. The meaning of a text is more complex, involving the relationship of one text to another (its intertextuality), one event to another (the historical context), and the social relationships of readers, teachers, peers, and others (the interpersonal context). Some literary theorists have suggested that there is no meaning *per se* and that all meanings can be deconstructed into nothingness. Some sociological theorists (often referred to as poststructuralists) have suggested that meaning is inherently unstable, incomplete and always political.

The consequences of these new theories for reading research and education are still unclear, except that they have caused many people to question the utility of the concept of **comprehension**. Do comprehending a text and understanding a text mean the same thing? Some people define comprehending a text as getting a meaning for or from the text, while understanding a text means learning about how a particular text is used, what it is used for, what meanings people give and have given to the text, and what interests they've had in doing so. Do learning to comprehend and learning to read mean the same thing? Some people define learning to comprehend as learning how to get meaning for and from a wide variety of texts, while learning to read means learning how to use texts effectively in a wide variety of social situations. Does **comprehension** equate with reading? Some people define **comprehension** as a psychological process, something an individual does, an internal mental activity, while others define reading as a social activity in which people (perhaps collectively) use written language in order to accomplish social, economic, cultural and political objectives.

As we noted at the beginning of this entry, although **comprehension** is a process, the process has been nominalised as a noun. Whether **comprehension** is defined as a cognitive process or a social process, to comprehend is to take action, to act upon the world. As we stated in the Introduction, by transforming a process (an action, a verb) into a thing (a noun), the action or process may be turned into a commodity that can be counted, measured, owned, marketed and distributed. The nominalisation of **comprehension** can perhaps be viewed as having suffered from becoming a commodity. Reading tests measure **comprehension** and teachers and experts tell pupils whether their **comprehension** is correct, which seems similar to the teachers and experts owning **comprehension**. Reading education becomes a way for pupils to acquire the skills to comprehend, which can be viewed as the distribution or marketing of **comprehension**.

Reference
E.B. Huey (1908) *The psychology and pedagogy of reading.* New York: Macmillan.

Curriculum (The reading curriculum)

From the Latin *curr-ere,* meaning 'to run', and *curricul,* meaning running, a running course, a race (*Oxford English Dictionary,* Vol. 11C, 1970, p. 1271). The Latin sense can be detected in **reading curricula,** which are often presented as a series of steps or a sequence of skills or competences to be covered.

On my desk before me is a book of 350 pages. It is called *Mønsterplan for Grunnskolen* – literally, *Model Plan for the Foundation School* (1971). I was able to buy it in a bookshop in Oslo. It is the **curriculum** of the Norwegian comprehensive school. It lays down the ground to be covered and to some extent the methods to be used for each subject in each year of the school. It also makes statements about aims. Such a document is not untypical of centralized school systems; and it is the response of such systems to the problem of ensuring regularity in the **curriculum.** One might call it a specification.

To the British teacher such an approach to the **curriculum** is quite novel. But in some countries the first thing that comes to mind when mention is made of the **curriculum** is a book of instructions to teachers. 'Could you please pass me the **curriculum,**' one might almost say.

Such a view equates the **curriculum** with a written prescription of what it is intended should happen in schools.

Some, however, equate the **curriculum** less with the intentions of the school than with its performance ... For such a **curriculum** one does not look at a book but at the school. If **curriculum** is defined in this way, then the study of **curriculum** can be reduced to the empirical study of schools. The **curriculum** is not the intention or prescription but what happens in real situations. It is not the aspiration, but the achievement...

We appear to be confronted by two different views of the **curriculum.** On the one hand the **curriculum** is seen as an intention, plan or prescription, an idea about what one would like to happen in schools. On the other it is seen as the existing state of affairs in schools, what does in fact happen. And since neither intentions nor happenings can be discussed until they are described or otherwise communicated, **curriculum** study rests on how we talk or write about these two ideas of **curriculum.**

Lawrence Stenhouse (1975)

An introduction to curriculum research and development

London: Heinemann Educational Books, pp. 1–2

What I mean by **curriculum** is the shaping of understanding, beliefs and values which goes on under the aegis of a school. Undoubtedly teachers' objectives, and their choices of content and method, are important, but they do not by any means constitute the whole. The pupils too have 'objectives', beliefs and values which must influence the effective **curriculum** just as much as do the teacher's planned objectives, since the 'shaping of understanding' which I mentioned above is largely their reshaping of existing knowledge. Moreover, every school has organizational and cultural characteristics, so that every teacher brings to the classroom both his [*sic*] version of the school's implicit values, and covert beliefs and assumptions of his own. These implicit goals and beliefs go as far to shape the effective **curriculum** as do the objectives to which the teacher would give deliberate assent. To understand how these unite to shape the social order of a classroom and thence what children learn, we need the intermediate concept of 'communication', which is common both to the public, shared ordering of belief and to the private ordering of belief by individuals. Here a 'psychological' model of learning is not enough: for **curriculum** theory a social model is needed, for it must acknowledge both learner and social milieu, and include communication from pupil to teacher as well as vice versa.

Douglas Barnes (1976)
From communication to curriculum
London: Penguin, pp. 187–8

Development (Reading development)

The metaphor of **development** occupies an interesting position in the evolution of the language for the teaching of reading. At the time it began to be widely used, it represented a principled challenge to the then dominant metaphors of 'acquisition' and 'attainment'. The adoption and use of the term **reading development** therefore reflects a need to find a nominalised term for 'learning to read' which is professionally and ideologically acceptable, while at the same time conveying academic and scientific respectability. Like many terms which have been self-consciously adopted in order to challenge common-sense assumptions, it's difficult to know whether the term **reading development** reflected an emerging consensus about the inadequacy and undesirability of earlier terms, or whether the term was deliberately promulgated as a kind of linguistic Trojan Horse to effect changes in thinking and behaviour.

The meanings, values and debates surrounding certain critical terms in the vocabulary for the teaching of reading often run in parallel with, and sometimes explicitly mimic, the meanings, values and debates surrounding similar terms in the vocabulary for studying spoken language and/or psychology. **Reading development** is a good example of this somewhat parasitic relationship: the history of **reading development** displays many of the same features as the history of the terms 'language development' and 'child development'.

It's worth noting Michael Halliday's views (1978, p. 16) on the undesirability of the term 'language acquisition' in the context of the study of spoken language:

> ...the learning of the mother tongue is often referred to as 'language acquisition'. This seems rather an unfortunate term because it suggests that language is some kind of commodity to be acquired, and, although the metaphor is innocent enough in itself, if it is taken too literally the consequences can be rather harmful. The use of this metaphor has led to the belief in what is known as a 'deficit theory' of language learning, as a means of explaining how children come to fail in school: the suggestion that certain children, perhaps because of their social background, have not acquired enough of this commodity called language, and in order to help them we must send relief supplies. The implication is that there is a gap to be filled, and from this derive various compensatory practices that may be largely irrelevant to the children's needs. Now this is a false and misleading view of language and of educational failure; and while one should not make too much of one item of terminology, we prefer to avoid the term 'language acquisition' and return to the earlier and entirely appropriate designation of 'language development'.

Halliday's analysis sheds some light on the reason why the term **reading development** is generally acceptable to most mainstream sensibilities. The term **development** carries with it progressive, child-centred and anti-mechanistic connotations.

If **reading development** is merely an interesting stage in a long-term search for a nominalised term for 'learning to read', then it's worth speculating about the kinds of terms which might replace it and the aspects of learning to read covered by **development**. 'Emergent reading' is one possibility, but this is not quite an exact alternative. It is too specifically associated with very young children, whereas **reading development** implictly relates to a longer age span. **Reading development** (like 'language development' and 'child development') has fairly strong Piagetian overtones. It conjures an image of the active, meaning-seeking child. But it also suggests a somewhat rigid and linear journey, punctuated by regular and predictable 'stages', and a journey made by a lone traveller discovering new knowledge and understanding by working in considerable isolation. The term **development** also has strong associations with childhood, which make it somewhat inappropriate to use to discuss the 'learning to read' of older children and adults.

The questions to ask about **development** and whatever terms later supplant it are:

- How does it explicitly and implicitly define learning to read? What ideological and practical work does it accomplish that 'learning to read' does not?

- How does it explicitly and implicitly define 'reading' and the 'reader'? Within what spheres of activity, disciplines and discourses does it locate 'reading' and the 'reader'?

- How does the term define the change from childhood to adulthood? What significance does it claim for 'learning to read' in this process of change?

Reference
Michael Halliday (1978) *Language as social semiotic: the social interpretation of language and meaning.* London: Edward Arnold.

Dyslexia

> [The term 'dyslexia'] is now used in common parlance only for those who we think ought to be able to read but can't. We don't say babies are dyslexic although we say some actresses are. We don't say people who have never been to school and haven't learned to read are dyslexic, we say that they are illiterate or semiliterate as the case may be.
>
> *Peter Young and Colin Tyre (1983)*
> Dyslexia or illiteracy? Realizing the right to read
> *Milton Keynes: The Open University Press, p. 20*

Dyslexia is a good example of the tendency, within the teaching of reading, to import (or to invent) medical (or pseudo-medical) terminology. **Dyslexia** invokes the discourse of the world of medicine first of all at the linguistic level, with its solemn Greek derivation and its associations with a number of (other) medical conditions; and secondly at the level of educational practice, with its strong suggestion of pathology, complex origins and clinical diagnosis and treatment.

The prefix *dys-* derives from the Greek prefix *dus-* meaning bad or difficult. *Lexia* derives from the Greek word *lexis*, meaning word. The term would technically mean 'bad word' or 'difficult word', if it weren't for the suffix *-ia*, which is used in both Greek and Latin as a way of forming nouns (that is, it is a nominalisation device). The *-ia* suffix is used widely in medical and psychological pathology (e.g. anaemia, pneumonia, schizophrenia), in botany (e.g. dahlia, fuchsia) and in geography (e.g. Australia, India). Literally, then, **dyslexia** means *the state of having difficulty with words*. It is one of a class of words which use the prefix *dys-* to denote badness or difficulty, such as dyspepsia (indigestion), dysphoria (a state of mental discomfort, the opposite of euphoria), dystopia (an imaginary place where everything is as bad as possible, the opposite of utopia) and dysuria (painful urination).

Implicit in the term **dyslexia** are some interesting mis-matches. First, there is the mis-match between the term's highly technical aura (suggesting scientism, precision and lack of ambiguity) and the utter lack of consensus over its meaning amongst practitioners and researchers. Second, there is the mis-match between the generality of the term's literal meaning ('difficulty with words') and the extraordinary specificity of the condition it was constructed to represent (which we can try to represent as 'reading, writing and/or spelling achievement significantly below general intellectual or spoken language ability, allegedly due to an ocular, neurological or aural disability').

All of these qualities contribute to the way the term **dyslexia** functions, both within educational circles and more widely. **Dyslexia** is not a description of a set of observable behaviours or attitudes, although it is often used as a kind of shorthand for a set of observable behaviours or attitudes. The term is used to represent a condition, implying that it can be confidently recognised if certain specific symptoms are present.

But this obscures the fact that there is no widespread consensus about diagnosis, aetiology or treatment (to use the medical terms this word invites); indeed, there is considerable disagreement. A term like anaemia, for example, simply means 'a deficiency of red blood cells'. There is a simple test to determine whether, and to what extent, the condition exists in a person. Unlike **dyslexia**, the diagnosis of anaemia in itself doesn't determine the cause of the condition. A diagnosis of **dyslexia** is a statement of suspected cause. No reliable test exists for determining whether a person 'has it', except in a very narrow sense: if the definition of **dyslexia** is no more than 'reading, writing and/or spelling achievement significantly below general intellectual or spoken language ability', then it is true that most people who have worked with children and/or adults still in the process of learning to read would recognise that some people appear to display this kind of mis-match. However, the question must be asked: why call this mis-match **dyslexia**? Does the term **dyslexia** bring us closer to an understanding of this mis-match, or why it should occur, or what can be done to reduce it? And why adopt a term which so zealously imitates the discourse of medical and psychological pathology?

By applying the term **dyslexia** to a child or adult who has been 'observed' to have a mis-match between their 'reading, writing and/or spelling achievement and their general intellectual or spoken language ability', much more is being done than simply and neutrally summarising that observation. The term explicitly and unabashedly problematises certain people in terms of their abnormality and ineffectuality. The use of the term **dyslexia** suggests:

- that the full range of methodologies conventionally available to education professionals have not worked where they would normally be expected to work;

- that we suspect there is something highly specific and technical wrong with the person;

- that it is time for the experts to take over.

In this way a particular kind of person is removed from the educational sphere, and relocated to a medical/clinical one. Indeed, the institutional environments to which such people are removed are often called 'clinics', which reinforces the medical metaphor.

The term **dyslexia** therefore has the effect of 'normalising' educational practice, since it implies that those who do not respond to the reading programmes offered within mainstream educational practice are qualitatively different from everyone else. The problem is located in the aberrance of the individual reader, rather than in the narrow definitions of 'reading' and 'learning to read' underlying educational practices.

And yet it is the very ambiguity of the term **dyslexia** which gives it its appeal. The term relieves the teacher of a burden of responsibility (both for causing the problem and for solving it), since there is no way that she or he could be expected to have prevented or treated this condition.[1] And although the problem is located within the learner, it is not a problem that the learner can be held responsible for, since those with **dyslexia** (increasingly called *Dyslexics*) are neither 'lazy' nor 'thick'. The term removes responsibility from the educational sphere to the medical one, validates educational practice as a standard against which people can be judged as normal or aberrant, and reinforces the prestige of the medical/technical over other kinds of metaphors.

Note

[1] This is not to say that some teachers don't feel de-skilled and disempowered as a result.

Failure and success (Failure and success in reading)

Examine the pictures and graphics below (a) to (g) and then complete the following sentence by choosing the best picture:

Failure is:

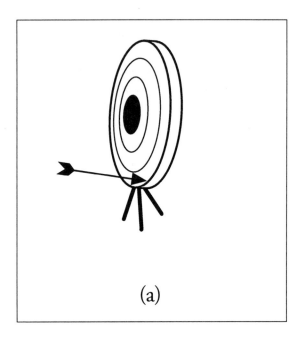

(a)

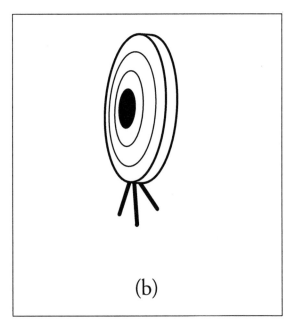

(b)

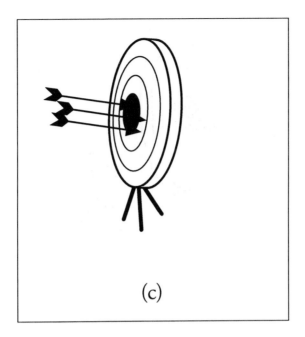

(c)

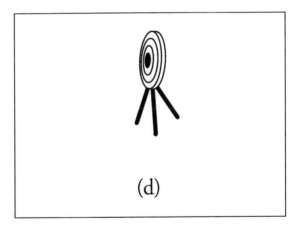

(d)

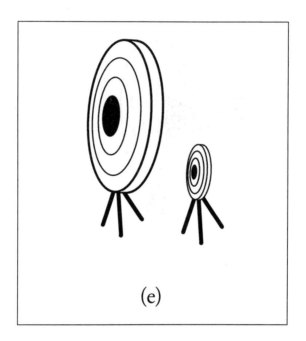

(e)

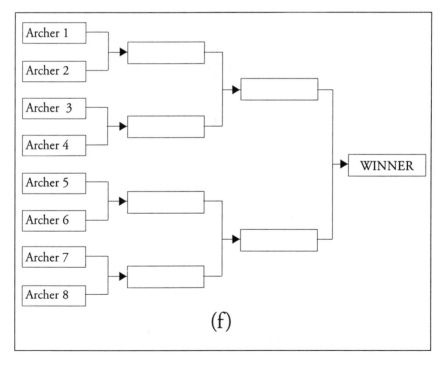

(f)

NONE OF THE ABOVE

The **failure** of children to learn to read causes great worry among teachers, parents and children as well. Even the potential of **failure** causes concern. Children who are failing to learn to read, and even those who are suspected of failing to learn to read in the future, are often sent to remedial reading classes where they recover from **failure** as if recovering from a disease. Children who fail to learn to read are often stigmatised and labelled, but so terrible is the label of **failure** that euphemisms are used. They are called 'remedial readers', 'slow readers', 'reluctant readers' or 'at risk', among others. Children who persist in failing to learn to read are often diagnosed as special needs children, relabelled as learning disabled, mentally disabled or dyslexic, and may be segregated from others. Adults who have not learned how to read are defined as illiterate and programmes and policies are designed to save them from their illiterate condition and presumed pitiful and impoverished lives, as if they have fallen from a state of grace.

Although medical and religious terms are often used in describing aspects of **failure**, the overall metaphor from which **failure** is derived is hierarchy. Grades descend: A, B, C, D, E; instructional groups are often organised by ability to read (top, middle, low); one moves up from being a non-reader (including both those who are unable to read and those who do not read) to a reader. One of the implications of the hierarchy is that higher locations are inherently defined as more desirable and are associated with greater privilege, power and rewards. Lower locations on the hierarchy – and the closer one is to **failure** – are not just associated with a lack of privileges but people so located are subject to various treatments and interventions. The major privilege of a higher location on the learning to read hierarchy is exclusion from the treatments, interventions and labels of lower social status that are given to those lower on the hierarchy. It is because of the hierarchy's orientation to **failure** that **failure** becomes the superordinate concept and the concepts of success and achievement become subordinate ones; and therefore it is appropriate to discuss **success** under the headword **failure**.

Success
What does it mean to be a **successful** reader? What does it mean to have a **successful** reading? What does it mean to have **success** at reading? We have identified at least five uses of **success**.

1. **Success** as an antonym of **failure**. Many uses of **success** and **failure** in the teaching of reading require that **success** and **failure** be antonyms and co-present, as in 'Success is the avoidance of **failure**' and in '90 per cent of the students were **successful** in passing the reading test'.

2. **Success** as a measure of standards. **Success** is often determined by meeting a standard, as in 'The student has **successfully** passed the standard required for reading' or 'The student has failed to pass the standard required for reading'.

3. **Success** as an outcome of competition. Inherently, competition defines **success**. Competition defines what counts as **success** and how much **success** there will be, as in 'Of the two thousand students who compete for the scholarship only five scholarships will be awarded'. In addition, **success** as competition also defines who is eligible to be considered for **success**, as in 'Only those students who received a 90 or above in their junior school reading test are allowed to compete for the scholarship'. By limiting who is eligible to compete for **success**, social groups and identities are created. But limitations are not created only by test makers and officials, but also by those who might participate in the competition, as in 'Mary did not take the scholarship test because she does not want to be called a boffin'. **Success** as an outcome of competition, then, is also a statement of social group member-ship and identity, and a hierarchical structuring of identity and membership.

4. **Success** as social acceptability. **Success** and **failure** are often used to indicate social acceptability, as in 'Amy has **successfully** adjusted to the new reading group we placed her in'; 'Tom has failed to adjust to his new reading group'.

5. **Success** as complementary to **failure**. As in, 'Tom learned through his **failures** to be a **success** in reading' or 'You can only be a **successful** reader if you are willing to risk **failure**'.

Each of the five uses of **success** describes a 'state of being' – a person is **successful**. Interestingly, that phrase does not have an analogue with **failure** – we do not say that a person is **failure**ful, although we can always say that a person has failed a lot or that a person is a **failure**. But those analogues are not states of being, unlike the state of being **successful**. To say that a person has failed a lot does not place the person in a state of being but rather gives a history that, hopefully, will be reversed. To say that a person is a **failure** is to define the person; it is the analogue of saying that a person is a **success**. In both cases, the person is defined. The transformation from **success** as a state of being to **success** as a kind of person is a part of a system of thought which suggests that some people exist in a state of being – being **successful** – because they are a **success**. Their **success** is not an attribute of conditions but an attribute of themselves. Similarly, being a **failure** is part of that same system of thought – **failure** is not a condition into which people fall but rather it is an attribute of people – the people who fail – and is located within them. So it is with being a **successful** reader or a **failure** at reading.

Answers to the question posed in the test at the beginning of this entry

(a)   The arrow has missed the bullseye but hit the target. Is hitting the target but missing the bullseye a failure?

(b)   Does having a target define failure?

(c)   Several arrows have hit the bullseye; one has missed the target completely. Does hitting the bullseye indicate success or the failure to shoot at a more difficult target? Does missing one arrow negate the success of the others? Is the missed arrow the success and are the other arrows the failures? If the missed arrow is viewed as errant, can any amount of previous success change the fact that the missing arrow is a failure.

(d)   Is failure defined by the size of the target?

(e)   Is failure defined by who gets to shoot at which target?

(f)   Is failure defined by the structure of competition?

(g)   Is failure defined by refusing to play? By refusing to put oneself at risk of failure?

Functional reading

Functional reading is a rather odd term, since it's difficult to imagine reading that isn't functional. *Whenever* we read, it serves a function, even if it is to stave off boredom, or to avoid being told off by a teacher, or to cheer ourselves up, or to satisfy our curiosity, or to neutralise insomnia. *Whatever* it is we read, reading it serves a function, even if it is junk mail, or the back of a newspaper in an unfamiliar foreign language held by someone on the train. Whether we read for work or pleasure, for information or recreation, our reading is functional.

So, if all reading is functional, why is there a separate and special category of reading called **functional reading** which has a prominent place in the discourse of reading pedagogy? Part of the reason for this is that the 'functional' in **functional reading** isn't used to mean 'useful' or 'purposeful', in the way that we've used it in the first paragraph, but rather 'necessary in order to function adequately in adult life'. **Functional reading** is therefore used to describe the literacy equivalent of the poverty line: the amount of reading ability needed in order to survive in the modern world. In fact, 'survival reading' has sometimes been used as a cognate term. But what must one be able to read in order to be capable of **functional reading**? The Bullock Report, in its discussion of **functional reading**, includes 'recipes, "social pamphlets", tax return guides, claims for industrial injuries, national insurance guides for married women, and most of the Highway Code' (para. 2.2). But for whom is this reading functional? And why these texts and not others? How well must the texts be read in order for the reading to be functional (assuming that this could be determined)? Clearly, any attempt to define, or to set out criteria for determining, **functional reading** encounters the same sets of imponderables as any attempt to define literacy (or illiteracy) itself. Although it has been argued that **functional reading** is every child's minimum entitlement, and it is every school's duty to provide it, the preoccupation with minimums, together with the reductionism and utilitarianism of most definitions of functional literacy, can quickly transform what was intended as a floor into a very low ceiling.

Functional reading, within the discourse of reading pedagogy, has an inferior status compared with whatever reading it is that people do above and beyond **functional reading**. There is therefore an implied hierarchy of reading types. **Functional reading** is at the bottom, and reading which has no material effect but is generally improving is at the top. Attached to this hierarchy is an ascending scale of moral value and moral benefit. The economic metaphor used earlier – suggesting that **functional reading** is the literacy equivalent of the poverty line – is apt here too. The reading that people do above **functional reading** is analogous to the goods and services people buy if their means are above the level of economic survival. So, in the same way that people with disposable capital in excess of their basic survival requirements attend the ballet, travel abroad and buy fine wines, people who have excess literacy capital dispose of it by doing reading which is superior to **functional reading**.

Thus, in most contexts, there is an implied 'merely' preceding **functional reading**. **Functional reading** is the reading that enables you to get by, but only if you can expect little more than to get by. Ultimately, then, **functional reading** describes the reading done by people who can do no more than functionally read. People who are able to do more than functionally read do not, by implication, ever read functionally, since they are able to read more than functionally.

Instruction (Reading instruction)

Dave: Barry, you and I have had different experiences with the word **instruction** that seem to reflect differences between the UK and the US. In the US, **instruction** and **reading instruction** may be the most frequently used terms in the whole vocabulary for the teaching of reading.

Barry: Really? Not in the UK, they aren't. **Instruction** is a term that is very rarely used in the British context. Not only is it rarely used, but I think for most British teachers it has quite explicit American overtones of programmed learning, of highly mechanistic conceptions of curriculum, teaching and learning. In fact, I don't think it's a term that would be tolerated by many British teachers – certainly not in relation to reading, or even any kind of language or English work in British schools. It's very rarely used in the professional literature, very rarely used in in-service work with British teachers. In fact, I think British teachers only come into contact with the term **instruction** when they read things written by Americans – you know, if they happened to pick up a copy of a journal like *The Reading Teacher* they would find the use of the term **reading instruction** quite a curious and foreign usage. Quite amused, probably, that the Americans would use such a mechanistic term.

Dave: Where is the term **instruction** used in Britain?

Barry: It would be in much more highly-structured skill contexts, like 'driving **instruction**' – you have a driving instructor when you're learning to drive. You might have a riding instructor if you're learning to ride a horse. In other words, practical skills where you're taken through a well-developed and highly-structured sequence of steps leading to competence.

               If you were going to unpack the term **instruction** with a group of American teachers, how would you start?

Dave: I'd start by unpacking the several meanings or senses of **instruction**. There are at least two kinds of meanings, I think. The first kind of meaning is like a programme, or a set of activities, or even a set of resources, that a teacher or a school might use. Someone might say: 'The school gives **instruction** in reading' or 'The child takes **instruction** in reading'.

Barry: So it's almost a euphemism for 'curriculum'?

Dave: No. I don't think so. Not at least as I've seen the word used by many teachers, schools administrators and others involved in education. One of the interesting things about the word **instruction** is that it's frequently separated from curriculum. So you have 'curriculum and **instruction**'.

Barry: Curriculum is the content 'out there', and **instruction** is the delivery of it?

Dave: Yes, traditionally speaking. Curriculum is what you teach; and **instruction** is how you teach. **Instruction** is the technology. I think probably what has happened to many teachers – particularly with regard to **reading instruction** – is that they are limited to the area of **instruction**. They are supposed to be experts in how to deliver the curriculum. Others define the curriculum: specialists, school boards, administrators, reading schemes. Teachers get defined as technologists and technicians who deliver the curriculum.

Barry: How is that distinct from 'pedagogy'?

Dave: The word 'pedagogy' isn't used much in the US.

Barry: What was the other meaning for **instruction**?

Dave: The sense of offering **instruction** itself. It's an educational programme that almost exists without pupils. You can have an **instruction**al programme – never mind who the pupils are.

Barry: So it's not interactive, it's a performance.

Dave: **Instruction** is like a commodity. You could talk about 'selling **instruction**' – 'we sell karate **instruction**'. Schools sell **reading instruction**. It's a commercial exchange of a kind. An interesting assumption is that if you work yourself up through the complete programme of **instruction**, you're assumed to have learned. So there's an equation between **instruction** and learning, which I think is often a false assumption to make.

Barry: So there's a kind of mis-match between what the teacher does when the teacher instructs or gives **instruction**, and any notion of what the child takes away, or interaction between teacher and child? There's no interactive quality to it when it's conceptualised like this.

Dave: Not when **instruction** is a noun, no; not as a noun. Contrast the sentences:
'The teacher instructs.'
'The teacher teaches.'
They don't have the same connotations – at least not for me, and probably not for a lot of people. 'The teacher instructs' sounds more directive, sounds more controlling, sounds less concerned with the 'what' of teaching, less concerned with the curriculum and less concerned with the pupil. When we say 'The teacher teaches', that – at least for me – has associations that are broader, more professionally-oriented associations, associations with both the 'what' and the 'how', and assumes much more emphasis on an interaction with pupils, much more open to flexibility in what happens. **Instruction** itself seems to me to be much more rigid, predetermined.

Barry: We need to think about how we're going to handle such widely differing understandings between US and UK audiences. The kind of distinctions we made between teaching and **instruction** would probably be recognised by both audiences, but the term **instruction** itself is so much more widely used and in that sense is relatively unproblematical in the American context. It's very rarely used, and is very highly problematical in the UK.

Dave: One of the questions we should ask is: What can we learn from the differences between the two cultures in their use of this term? I think it's very useful to have the term made problematical by looking at how it's treated in different countries. It's one of the ways we can learn from each other. At the same time it's important to think about what gets problematised when a term is not used in a particular society.

Barry: The existence, prominence and various meanings of the two terms may tell us something about the struggles that are going on in reading education both in the US and the UK. The resistance to a term like **instruction** in the UK might well signify a kind of an anti-mechanistic movement, particularly in primary education and in English teaching. Even though **instruction**, in the sense that you and I understand it, may be what's going on in at least some classrooms here.

Motivation

> **Motivation is a word we've invented to fill a gap we've created.**
>
> *James Britton*
>
> *(personal communication)*

In the teaching of reading **motivation** is primarily used to express concern about students who are not motivated to read or to learn to read. Questions are typically asked about how a student can be motivated to read. And typically the answers focus on providing **motivation** (rewards for reading), appealing to the pupil's inherent **motivation** (providing books that appeal to the pupil's interests) or on improving the pupil's character (counselling the pupil to develop intrinsic **motivation** to read).

The question 'How to motivate a student to read?' emphasises the action of *motivating*, a transitive verb, doing something to someone. The answers transform the verb – *motivate* – into a noun, a quality that a pupil either has or doesn't have. When defined as a noun, teachers are viewed as creating **motivation** and then giving it to their pupils. By transforming *motivate* into a noun, the agency involved in **motivation** is neutralised. **Motivation** is not defined as somebody doing something to someone, but as a commodity that pupils can have lots or little of. As a quantity, pupils can be held accountable for having or not having sufficient **motivation** to read, and teachers can be held accountable for not providing enough **motivation**.

It is interesting to contrast **motivation** and desire. Desire is associated with passion, romance, love and sex. Desire has substance. Even when desire is used metaphorically – 'I hope you will have a desire to read the book' – desire nonetheless carries a sense of passion and sexual energy. We often speak of the content and characters of books as showing desire and passion: the desires of Ursula and Gudrun in D.H. Lawrence's *Women in love*, the passion of Celie in Alice Walker's *The color purple*, or the desires of Henry Fielding's *Tom Jones*. By contrast, readers are not conceived of as having desire and passion; instead they have **motivation**. Desire and passion are kept textual and fictional. By stripping students of desire and renaming it **motivation**, the task of getting people to do something, like reading – whether it is something they want to do themselves or something others want them to do – becomes a technological task rather than a moral and political one involving the full range of human emotions, desires and passions.

Phonics

There are few debates in education that are more acrimonious than the debate over **phonics**. Teachers, researchers, politicians and parents argue about whether explicit teaching of the relationship between the sounds of the language and its written symbols is an effective way to promote reading development. Or perhaps more accurately, the argument has been whether methods of teaching reading that eschew **phonics** are effective.

According to some historians of the teaching of reading, **phonics** supplanted the alphabetic method where children called out the names of letters and then said the word: es-pee-oh-tee, Spot. With **phonics**, children sounded out the letters, saying the sound of each letter and then blending them together.

There has been a series of scientific studies on the explicit teaching of **phonics**, comparing it to other methods of teaching reading. The results have not only been inconclusive but also unhelpful and often hurtful. For example, in the early 1960s a series of co-ordinated studies on the teaching of beginning reading, known popularly as the *First Grade Studies,* was sponsored by the US government. Overall, the studies showed no one particular method of teaching reading was by itself superior to another. The scholars in charge of co-ordinating the studies reported their 'no findings' in a straightforward manner. There are a number of reasons why the *First Grade Studies* may have had such overall findings: inadequate methods, inadequate research design (overall conception of the research), researcher bias (studies were conducted by researchers with a broad range of differing perspectives), among other problems. It may even be that method of instruction – formally defined – does not make a statistical difference in reading achievement tests. Recent approaches to teaching reading developed since the mid-1960s – such as 'whole language' and the use of 'real books' – were not included, of course. Despite the false logic, some people argued that the *First Grade Studies* have proved that no one way of teaching reading is better than another and some have pushed the argument even further claiming that how one teaches reading is irrelevant. Conversely, some researchers, teachers and politicians have extracted selective studies from the *First Grade Studies* and elsewhere to 'prove' their point of view. Since the *First Grade Studies* there has been a continuing series of 'scientific' studies purporting to prove one side of the debate or another. In the current debate about the teaching of reading, advocates of various positions hurl research studies at each other almost as frequently as they hurl insults.

The debate over the teaching of **phonics** has been joined by politicians, political interest groups and the general public. The failure of teachers to teach **phonics** explicitly, to emphasise **phonics** first in reading instruction, is occasionally associated with the decline of standards and academic achievement, the lack of discipline in schools, newfangledness, a lack of traditional values in schools, and with the perceived overall moral, educational and economic decay of society. Even if one were to believe that there is an overall decay of society, it is hard to believe that teaching children **phonics** would remedy the decay. Yet the vehemence of attacks on teachers and others who eschew the explicit teaching of **phonics** would lead one to believe so.

The debate over **phonics** also has an economic side. A great deal of money is spent by schools on beginning reading materials. Schools will purchase those materials that best represent their views on **phonics**. In some cases, purchases are made based on how the materials will look to people outside the classroom – parents and the general public. The profits of some publishing companies may depend on how their materials package **phonics**. Some publishing companies may carry educational materials with very different perspectives on beginnning reading, from a very heavy **phonics** emphasis to no **phonics**, in order to sell to a broader range of schools. But in addition to sales to teachers, there is a growing market of materials for teaching **phonics** directed at parents. Such marketing is only possible because of folk beliefs about the importance of explicit **phonics** teaching and the impression created by various political interest groups and others that children are failing to learn to read because teachers are not teaching **phonics**.

The debate over **phonics** is remarkable for how it has saturated the public discourse on education, how it has become associated with broader political and ideological positions, and the degree of passion involved in the debate. But it is also remarkable for the lack of definition. **Phonics** is one of the few words that has no meaning outside the teaching of reading. But what is **phonics**?

The word **phonics** consists of two morphemes: *phone* and *-ics*. In the current debate about how best to teach reading, the emphasis may seem to be concerned with the first morpheme, *phone* – the sounds of the language. Is sounding out words an effective way to read? But in reality the debate is much more about the second morpheme, *-ics*.

-ics is a suffix based on the suffix *-ic* which is derived from Greek and then Latin, primarily used in forming various types of adjectives, meaning 'in the manner of'.[1] Although used in a broad range of academic and non-academic terms (like *scholastic* and *sarcastic*) *-ic* has often been associated with scientific terms (like *sulphuric acid*). But *-ic* is also found in nouns, such as *music* and *critic*, perhaps deriving from the Greek use of such terms to stand for subjects and the names of various arts, a *critic* being a person who is critical, *music* being the arts of the muses. The names of sciences, before 1500, were often *-ic* as in *mathematic* and *physic* where later they became *-ics* as in *mathematics* and *physics* although they remained singular nouns. The exact etymological history of *-ics* is less important than the associations *-ics* has and the confusions it causes. Although not the only association, *-ics* is associated with scient*ic* discourse, academ*ics*, and with systemat*ic* procedures. It is an adjective – *phonic instruction* – that has become a noun – **phonics**. In becoming a noun it

takes on a presumed material reality, rather than being a quality or hue of something else. As discussed previously in the Introduction and in other entries, nominalisation makes it possible to own, distribute and market a phenomenon. In addition, the nominalisation of *phonic* gives it existence and allows it to be equated with reading. In effect, it can become a definition of reading only because it has been nominalised.

As a noun, **phonics** is used both as a plural and a singular. As a plural noun it refers to the rules that associate letters with sounds. As such, **phonics** is quantifiable, as in 'Does Sally know all her **phonics** [phonic rules]?' The plural nature of **phonics** allows the breakdown of grapho-phonemic system of a language (its sound–letter system) into a set of discrete parts and operations, and it allows the set of parts and operations to be used as a standard of measurement, as in 'John only knows half of his **phonics**' and 'Margaret knows her **phonics** for initial consonants but does not yet know how to work out vowel sounds and blends'. The description of letter-sound associations as rules suggests a system, discipline, a science. This is also suggested by the *-ics* suffix's association with scientific and academic discourse. The use of *-ics* here is as a singular, as in '**Phonics** *is* the only way to teach reading'. As a singular noun, **phonics** can take adjectives, as in *analytic phonics* and *synthetic phonics*, which allows debate over which type of **phonics** is better without necessarily questioning what **phonics** itself is. Further, as a singular noun, **phonics** can be placed in opposition to other methods of teaching reading as in, '**phonics** versus *real books*'. In so doing, **phonics** is politically positioned as a superordinate concept rather than either a component of other concepts of teaching and learning to read or a type of reading strategy.

The *-ics* in **phonics** ties reading to a market economy, justified as a scientific technology. Reading is equated with **phonics** without questioning what reading is or what **phonics** is. No wonder the acrimonious debate and the involvement of politicians and political interest groups. No wonder the appeal to scientific studies, attempting to treat **phonics** as a non-ideological and non-political entity.

Note
[1]Based on definition in the *Oxford English Dictionary* (1989) Oxford: Clarendon Press, pp. 595–6.

Reader

We have assembled a collection of quotations here, each of which casts the **reader** in a slightly different light, to show that **reader** is not a single or stable idea and to show how different theorists have conceptualised it. All emphases of the word **reader** are our own.

> On the whole, the meanings [of words] seemed usually to be felt as belonging to the larger wholes, to the sentences and other larger units. The words were mainly 'counters', felt as having a part in the total, but their function being mainly to help tide one over to a place where a new meaning would be suggested or completed. The **reader** seldom escaped feeling the particular words in a perspective of the before and after, and was often much puzzled, even baffled, to know how to deal with them as they stood with the total sense uncompleted. The absence of images, at least with the individual words, was rather marked.

> *Edmund Burke Huey (1968) (first published 1908)*
> The psychology and pedagogy of reading
> *Cambridge, Mass: MIT Press, pp. 158–9*

> ...the literary work has two poles, which we might call the artistic and the esthetic: the artistic refers to the text created by the author, and the esthetic to the realization accomplished by the **reader**. From this polarity it follows that the literary work cannot be completely identical with the text, or with the realization of the text, but in fact must lie half-way between the two. The work is more than the text, for the text only takes on life when it is realized, and furthermore the realization is by no means independent of the individual disposition of the **reader** – though this in turn is acted upon by the different patterns of the text. The covergence of text and **reader** brings the literary work into existence, and this convergence can never be precisely pinpointed, but must always remain virtual, as it is not to be identified either with the reality of the text or with the individual disposition of the **reader**.

> *Wolfgang Iser (1974)*
> The implied reader: patterns of communication
> in prose fiction from Bunyan to Beckett
> *Baltimore, Maryland: The Johns Hopkins Press, pp. 274–5*

'The Last Lesson'

FROM
MCGUFFEY'S
FIRST
ECLECTIC READER

làst   slātes   wrīte   wāste

nēat   tāk'en   clēan   learn

rēad'er   pàr'ents   sĕc'ond

We have come to the last lesson in this book. We have finished the First **Reader.**

You can now read all the lessons in it, and can write them on your slates.

Have you taken good care of your book? Children should always keep their books neat and clean.

Are you not glad to be ready for a new book?

Your parents are very kind to send you to school. If you are good, and if you try to learn, your teacher will love you, and you will please your parents.

Be kind to all, and do not waste time in school.

When you go home, you may ask your parents to get you a Second **Reader.**

(previous page)

William Holmes McGuffy. 'The Last Lesson From McGuffey's First Eclectic **Reader***' (no date given). Taken from Abraham Lass and Norma Tasman (eds)* (1980) Going to school: an anthology of prose about teachers and students. *New York: New American Library, pp. 279–80. (The large font and diacritical marks simulate the presentation given in the book; the bold type is our emphasis.)*

'So much fiction treats the **reader** like a randy ape,' she says severely. 'We have quite enough explicit sex; we don't need me. I want the **reader** to write those scenes, to have pleasure imagining the characters in bed, because they will do it better than me. I couldn't do it for toffee.'

Joanna Trollope, interviewed by Geraldine Bedell
in The Independent on Sunday, *27 June 1993, p. 16 of Review section*

Part of the difficulty with the **reader** in this series is that their texts are so truncated and condensed as to introduce only a few words at a time to children who are beginning to read.

Bruno Bettelheim and Karen Zelan (1981)
On learning to read: the child's fascination with meaning
London: Penguin Books, p. 163

The proper meaning of a passage (what it really means) is a kind of scholastic ghost with very much less in it than a good **reader** will rightly find there.

I.A. Richards (1943)
How to read a page
London: Routledge and Kegan Paul, p. 94

The writings of Marshall McLuhan are so compounded of novelty, force of suggestion, vulgarity of mind, and sheer carelessness that one is quickly tempted to put them aside. Many aspects of his success represent modern journalism at its most obvious. The McLuhan cult is characteristic of those confidence tricks of 'high journalism' which, perhaps more than any other force, deafen and cheapen the life of ideas. Yet all this is part of the point: the question of how to read McLuhan, of whether reading him is in itself an obsolescent mode of contact, is implicit in McLuhan's own work. The crises of relationship between traditional literacy and the hypnotic mendacities of the mass-media are exactly those to which McLuhan himself applies his rhetorical, confused, but often penetrating attention. 'Better written,' McLuhan's books and essays would be false to their implications. A McLuhan too fastidious or ironic to make use of the advertising powers of the mass-circulation magazines or the television interview would be negating his own principal argument. He sets his **reader** a perpetual, irritating problem: that of reading any further. But that is his master stroke: by making of his manner a close representation of the anomalies which he observes in the act of reading, in the essential nature of human communication, McLuhan draws us into his argument. To put him down is to let that argument pass unchallenged.

George Steiner (1970)
'On reading Marshall McLuhan (1963)' in
Language and silence: essays on language, literature and the inhuman
New York: Atheneum, p. 251

Thus is revealed the total existence of writing: a text is made of multiple writings, drawn from many cultures and entering into mutual relations of dialogue, parody, contestation, but there is one place where this multiplicity is focused and that place is the **reader**, not, as was hitherto said, the author. The **reader** is the space on which all the quotations that make up a writing are inscribed without any of them being lost; a text's unity lies not in its origin but in its destination. Yet this destination cannot any longer be personal: the **reader** is without history, biography, psychology; he is simply that someone who holds together in a single field all the traces by which the written text is constituted. Which is why it is derisory to condemn the new writing in the name of a humanism hypocritically turned champion of the **reader's** rights. Classic criticism never paid any attention to the **reader**; for it, the writer is the only person in literature. We are now beginning to let ourselves be fooled no longer by the arrogant antiphrastical recriminations of good society in favour of the very thing it sets aside, ignores, smothers, or destroys; we know that to give writing its future, it is necessary to overthrow the myth: the birth of the **reader** must be at the cost of the death of the Author.

Roland Barthes (1977)
'The death of the author' in Image, music, text
London: Fontana

The meanings of **readers** are only known through the texts that they construct, in specific conditions and contexts, in response to a designated text (among others). The meanings of writers are the traces and effects of innumerable prior acts of reading, realized only through text, again produced in specific contexts and conditions. **Readers** and writers are antagonistic and interdependent to different degrees, and no analysis can afford to forget either dimension.

Robert Hodge and Gunther Kress (1993) (first published 1979)
Language as ideology *(second edition)*
London: Routledge, pp. 175–6

Reader response

Perhaps the most famous use of 'response' has been in the stimulus–response theories of behaviourist psychology. Stimulus–response theories focus only on behaviour, on how a particular behaviour (response) might be linked to a particular stimulus. While not denying that mental activity occurred, they negated the importance of examining mental processes. Only the stimulus, the behaviour of the individual, and reinforcing conditions count. Human behaviour, including reading, was viewed as a series of stimulus–response chains, essentially amoral in nature.

Although also focused on response, reader-response theories define response not as behaviour but as mental responses, including the intellectual and emotional responses people have to what they read. The behavioural responses people make, what they say or write about what they read, are 'windows' for understanding their intellectual and emotional responses. Yet despite these profound differences there are many similarities.

Both reader-response theory and stimulus–response theory define written text as stimulus, and reading as response.

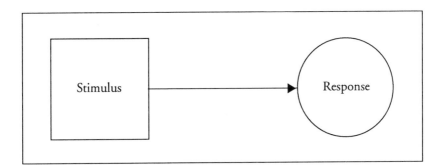

Both theories emphasise response as an attribute of the individual rather than viewing response as a social phenomenon. Both theories acknowledge that background factors and situational factors influence the nature of a response but subordinate these factors to the response itself. For example, both stimulus–response theories and reader-response theories would focus attention on the responses a pupil would make in a classroom. How did John respond to the story he read? How did his previous experiences affect his response? How did the conditions in the classroom influence his response? While the answers of stimulus–response theorists and reader-response theorists would be different, it is important to note that the questions are similar. The view of response suggested by such questions – whether derived from reader-response theory or stimulus–response theory, is different from viewing

John as part of a group and viewing his **response** as part of group behaviour, a group **response**, a social act. Why are the students in the year 8 class refusing to co-operate with the teacher in the discussion of the story they were reading? How are they orchestrating and co-ordinating their resistance so that it is more than the resistance of just individual students but the resistance of the class as a whole?

One of the ways that **reader-response** theories differ from stimulus–**response** theories is in the location of meaning. Stimulus–**response** theories focus only on behaviour; meaning is not an issue. **Reader–response** theories locate meaning in the interaction (called a transaction) between a reader and a text, as such meaning lies in neither the reader nor the text by themselves.

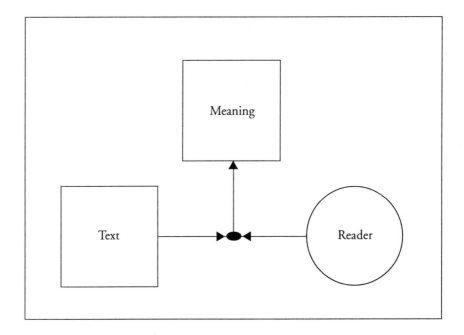

But where do the meanings that come into being through reader-text interaction reside? Many diagrams of reader–text transaction, like the one above, show these meanings residing in the ether.

From the perspective of **reader-response** theory, the new meanings and **responses** created through the transaction of a reader and a text are both intellectual and emotional. The deeper and more sophisticated the **response** the better. Various educational tasks may help the reader's **response** become deeper and more sophisticated, including activities such as discussions that explore preliminary **responses**, art work, writing, drama, among others. In addition, consideration can be given to the stimulus itself and the depth of **response** it is likely to evoke. Some written texts (e.g. stories) are better than others at evoking higher-quality **response**s, although there is not necessarily a formula for predicting which written texts will produce high-quality **response**s in which students in any specific situation. But the emphasis on a high-quality **response** puts pupils at least some of the time in a double-bind. On one hand, the **response**s they are encouraged to make should be 'genuine' **response**s that derive from their individual transaction with a text. On the other hand, some **response**s are more valued than others. The ability to produce valued **response**s – the background experiences and ways of transacting with written texts needed – can be viewed as part of the cultural capital that is unevenly distributed among pupils. In other words, some pupils have the background experiences and wherewithal to produce genuine (or seemingly genuine) **response**s that are valued by their teachers, while other pupils have few clues as to what is valued, how to create a valued **response** or how to make their **response** at least seem genuine.

Reader-response advocates often place themselves in opposition to traditional reading instruction. They privilege the intellectual and emotional **response**s made by the pupil to a written text instead of the pupil's performance on a test in which the correct answers are predetermined. The pupil's **response** is also privileged over the **response** desired by the teacher. For example, the teacher may want the pupil to feel sympathy for the protagonist in a book like *Flowers for Algernon*, but instead a pupil may view Charley, the protagonist, as humorous and have little sympathy for him.

Yet at least in practice if not in theory there is often slippage between privileging the pupil's **response** and shaping it. Techniques for deepening and improving the quality of pupil **response** often seem to lead to pupil **response**s that are similar to those desired by the teacher. Of course, since it is impossible for the teacher or any one to know what exactly is going on inside a pupil's mind, and the best that can be done is to make inferences from behaviour (such as a written essay or what is sometimes called a **response** journal), it may occur that pupils only provide the behaviour teachers desire while keeping other thoughts and feelings to themselves. No mechanism is provided in **reader-response** theory for critical analysis of the social dynamics involved in **response** production.

One question to ask of **reader-response** theory is: to what end is a reader's aesthetic, emotional or intellectual **response**? **Response** is usually viewed as an end in itself. This can lead to the accusation that **reader-response** theory reflects a 'consumerist' ideology or metaphor. Writing in 1928 about various literary theories, Mikhail Bakhtin and P.N. Medvedev argued that:

> The conception of a work of art as an object of individual pleasure and experience is
> essentially the expression of a tendency to equate an ideological phenomenon to a
> product of individual consumption.

However, the work of art, like every other ideological product, is an object of intercourse. It is not the individual, subjective psychic states it elicits that are important in art [or in reading], but rather the social connections, the interactions of many people it brings about.

M.M. Bakhtin and P.N. Medvedev
(first published 1928; trans. 1985)
The formal method in literary scholarship:
a critical introduction to sociological poetics
Cambridge, MA: Harvard University Press, p. 11

Bakhtin and Medvedev's criticism of literary theories, written sixty-six years ago, is still an important perspective from which to critique theories of reading, including **reader-response** theories. When all that matters is the reader's experience of **response**, this is a luxury that very few children can afford. And, to the extent that only the depth and quality of an individual's **response** is evaluated and not its context, content or implicit values, **reader-response** theory can be viewed, like stimulus–**response** theory, as amoral.

Readiness (Reading readiness)

Even in its everyday usage, the word **readiness** contains considerable ambiguity. We can envisage something or someone having **readiness** in both a passive and an active sense. We say that 'all is in **readiness**', conveying that preparations have been made and implying that the state of preparedness is the result of our own diligent efforts. We also use the word **readiness** to describe a willingness, or quickness, or resourcefulness, as in 'she was known for her **readiness** of wit in discussions' or 'her **readiness** in a crisis', suggesting a more inherent characteristic. In both senses, there are strong overtones of imminence and expectancy, of something about to happen.

In recent years, **readiness** has acquired a somewhat narrow meaning within the teaching of reading: it is frequently contrasted with 'emergence'. This oppositional relationship casts **reading readiness** as a concept based on the idea that certain specific kinds of visual and perceptual maturation have to take place before young children can profit from reading instruction, and that there is a stage at about the age of six when these conditions are in place. According to this view, there is a distinctive 'pre-reading phase', which precedes **readiness**, during which only a limited amount can be done by the teacher and/or parent to prepare the young child for their eventual initiation into reading. **Readiness** activities include, for example, inviting the child to take part in exercises which develop visual discrimination, left-to-right orientation and motor co-ordination. Reading to the child and widening the child's vocabulary are also considered to be generally beneficial **readiness** activities. However, it would not be fruitful, according to this view, to try to teach the child to read in the formal, technical sense before they have reached a state of **readiness**. Indeed, several people have suggested that this would actually be harmful. A range of '**reading readiness** tests' have been devised to help teachers to determine whether the critical stage of **readiness** has been reached. The active–passive dichotomy is therefore played out, in a limited sense, here: does the child become 'ready', or is the child made 'ready'?

In contrast, the term 'emergent' – as in 'emergent literacy' – emphasises the literacy learning accomplished by very young children through participation in purposeful, print-orientated activities in the home and elsewhere. This literacy learning consists of, for example, an awareness of the everyday functions which reading and writing serve, a developing sensitivity to the ways in which readers and writers behave and use print to achieve non-literate objectives, and a growing familiarity with the language of book-based stories. These kinds of learning, according to the 'emergent' view, begin at a very early age by virtue of the fact that all children in our society grow up within a print-orientated culture. Further, learning about the nature and uses of print is viewed as considerably more significant for very young children than either visual–perceptual development or formal instruction. However, it could be argued that by naming this process 'emergent reading', rather than just 'reading' or 'early reading', the two positions share a basic assumption that what very young children do is not yet reading, that reading is something that will happen in the future.

With the terms contrasted in this rather polarised way, **readiness** can be seen as an expression of a developmental psychological view of early reading, in which learning to read is closely linked with children's cognitive and physical maturation, and 'emergent' as an expression of a more holistic model, in which learning to read is closely linked with children's growing cultural knowledge. Ironically, **reading readiness** in the sense we have defined it here is considered to be a rather obsolete term even by those who advocate 'bottom-up' or 'skills' models and methods, but it is frequently cited by those arguing the 'emergent' position as the notion which 'emergence' has superseded. Hence, in the contemporary discourse of reading pedagogy, the term **readiness** is probably only meaningful in this specific oppositional context.

However, the term **readiness** only acquired this specific perceptual/visual meaning relatively recently. It has held a number of different positions in debates over early reading models and methods as the terms of those debates have changed. In general, the term represented the focus for a long-standing but more broadly-based debate over the age at which children should be taught to read. In fact, it is only relatively recently that this debate has ceased to dominate in reading circles. Huey (1908), in his seminal work on reading, argued that 'there would be little loss and often much gain if the child did not read much until his eighth year or later'. In this, Huey was drawing on Dewey's work on elementary education and was contributing to a debate which had started in the 1890s and continued in various guises for many years. A number of different ages, sometimes as old as ten, have been defended at various times. Huey's argument was based partly on theories of child development, but much of his tone was moral: formal teaching of reading was incompatible with his philosophy of education and conception of childhood. Huey's ideas in some ways anticipated the more recent work on emergent literacy.

The point here is that the term **readiness** has been used historically to argue for a delay to the teaching of reading from both a 'humanistic' perspective (in which such a delay was part of a protectiveness towards the young child) as well as a psychological perspective (in which a certain level of cognitive and perceptual development was seen as essential for instruction to be beneficial). In some usages, **readiness** merely denoted the point when children were able to respond to training in phonetic analysis, and so some phonics advocates dismiss the concept of **readiness** simply on the grounds that even very young children can profitably be introduced to the relationship between letters and sounds.

Whilst **readiness** has evolved through several mutations, it can nevertheless be argued that all of them are underpinned by a common assumption, that of a critical threshold. The assumption of a critical threshold can be contrasted with the principles underlying the emergent literacy position. The reluctance of emergent literacy advocates to comment on suitable ages for introducing children to various aspects of reading reflects the fact that, within this perspective, such a consideration is nonsensical, of little interest, and further demonstrates the contrast between this perspective and all senses in which the term **readiness** has been used. We are reliably informed that Jerome Bruner has somewhere called the concept of **readiness** 'a mischievous half-truth'.

Reference

E.B. Huey (1908) *The psychology and pedagogy of reading.* New York: Macmillan (quoted in Hunter Diack (1965) *In spite of the alphabet: a study of the teaching of reading.* London: Chatto & Windus).

Reading age

In view of the relatively recent advent of literacy in the history of human development, the uninitiated might be forgiven for assuming that the **Reading Age** is the term used by historians and archaeologists to refer to the present epoch, following on from the Ice Age, the Stone Age and the Bronze Age. It's not an entirely fanciful idea: the artefacts of our time will convey to people in the future the central role played by literacy in our culture and the diverse functions served by reading and writing to communicate and record ideas and information. In this sense, we *live* in the **Reading Age**.

However, this is not the meaning denoted by **reading age** for those initiated into the discourse of reading pedagogy. Simply put, **reading age** is used to signify a person's reading competence, expressed as the age for which that person's reading competence would be normal. In other words, a **reading age** of ten years can (according to the principles upon which the concept is based) be assigned to a person of any chronological age. Assigned to a person aged ten years, it signifies that the person's level of reading competence is normal for their age. Assigned to a person aged nine years, it signifies that the person's level of reading competence is comparable to the reading competence of an average ten-year-old and is therefore one year in advance of their chronological age. And assigned to a person aged eleven years, it signifies that the person's level of reading competence is one year behind their chronological age.

The origins of the term **reading age** lie in the early work of educational psychologists at the end of the nineteenth century. The notion of 'backwardness' was a source of considerable research interest – both in terms of general intellectual aptitude and more specifically in relation to reading. In this sense the concept of the **reading age** is closely linked with the development of the notion of 'intelligence' and 'IQ', and of the growth of psychometric principles governing the construction of standardised tests. **Reading age** therefore expressed a central principle in the then fledgeling field of the psychology of reading: that the reading competence of any individual could be represented by comparing it with the chronological age of a normally developing reader. Despite the many theoretical, technical and professional criticisms which have been made of the concept both within and outside the psychometric industry, the concept has been the principal unit of currency for expressing reading ability in the post-war period.

There are three theoretical assumptions underlying the concept of **reading age**, which are often taken for granted when the **reading age** is used or discussed but are worth making explicit:

1.   Reading development is closely linked to age, and is analogous to other age-related (and mainly physical) manifestations of maturation such as height, weight and so on.

It is claimed that, like these other age-related characteristics, reading ability is 'normally distributed' in any large population of people at a given age. That is, it will produce a typical bell-shaped curve, with the majority of people clustering around the norm and an equal number of people occupying positions at varying degrees of distance from the norm. The claim is that norms are produced empirically rather than driven by a normative model. That is to say that the normal distribution of reading ability in the population has been 'discovered' through observation and measurement rather than through statistical manipulation or pre-figured conclusions. However, the 'model' and the 'data' are now so mutually reinforcing that it is difficult to unpick cause from effect. As Denis Vincent (1974) has said: 'reading – at least in its quantitative aspects – is only associated with age fortuitously. Reading development lacks its Piaget, and until it can be described in the terms in which cognitive-developmentalists describe mental growth it will not have a true age-scale.'

Factors which, it may be argued, influence the rate of reading development (such as innate ability, home background, early acquaintance with reading/writing, motivation, age of school entry and kind and amount of teaching and reading experience at school and elsewhere) are essentially discounted or are at best introduced speculatively as explanatory variables. Certainly, **reading ages** are not statistically adjusted to take these factors into account. So, even though it is claimed that the values for 'normal reading' for different age-levels are calculated statistically from measured data – as opposed to being based on an abstract model – the notion that normal reading development is closely linked to normal maturation determines many of the methods used for calculating **reading ages**.

2.   Reading development follows the same linear course for all individuals, and individuals vary in their reading development only in the rate at which they follow that linear course relative to their chronological age.

In this way anyone's reading can be plotted on the same single line, regardless of their chronological age. A six-year-old with a **reading age** of seven years is therefore, for these purposes, directly comparable to a fifteen-year old with a **reading age** of seven years. Within the terms of this concept, there is nothing misleading or inadequate about representing the reading competence of a seven-year-old and the reading competence of a fifteen-year-old using exactly the same expression.

The irony is that a paradigm which is so wedded to the critical importance of age should ultimately assert the possibility of expressing a child's reading ability independently of age. There is therefore an in-built tension within the concept itself between age-related and age-independent expressions of reading ability. In its assumption that all readers develop along a standard pathway (but vary according to rate) the normative paradigm and the criterion-referenced paradigm share some important common ground, viz. that 'spiral' pathways or 'recursive' pathways, or pathways characterised by sharp rises followed by plateaux, are misleading representations of learning to read.

3.   Normal reading development advances in regular units of time which map squarely onto chronological progress – that is, the net progress made by a normal nine-year-old in the course of twelve months is comparable to the progress made by a normal sixteen-year-old during the same period.

Of course, in one sense this is uncontroversial, since in any twelve-month period all readers are a year older in their reading! However, this is not what is meant here. In fact, within the psychometric paradigm it is ultimately of no significance whether a sixteen-year-old makes the same amount of real reading progress in a year as a nine-year-old. What is signficant is that the amount of progress made in a year by a normal nine-year-old or a normal sixteen-year old is treated as a 'year's growth', and can therefore be treated as a standard unit irrespective of the actual amount of progress. In this respect time is spread out into standard units in much the same way that projections of the earth's surface manipulate its curvature in order to represent it in two dimensions. So, the fact that a sixteen-year-old who is two years 'behind' in his/her reading has less actual ground to make up than a nine-year-old who is two years 'behind' doesn't matter: what matters is that it would take a normal reader two years to accomplish either of them at the relevant age.

In addition to the theoretical assumptions underlying the concept of **reading age**, there are also assumptions underlying the methods used for calculating the **reading age** which are worth scrutinising. Essentially, one of two methods is used. First, there is the statistical/empirical approach, which involves either finding the average age for each score group, or finding the average score for each age group. In other words, one either identifies the average chronological age for the group achieving a particular score on the test, and uses that chronological age as the **reading age** value for that score, or one finds the average score for a particular age group, and uses the chronological age of the group as the **reading age** value for that score. Interestingly, according to Denis Vincent (1974), these two methods rarely produce the same result in the case of reading 'because age and reading test scores are not perfectly correlated'.

The alternative way is by calibration with an established measure for **reading age** such as a long-standing test. The circularity here is so obvious that it is surprising the method persists as strongly as it does. It means, of course, that the validation of reading tests simply serves to perpetuate a descending spiral of mutually-reinforcing assessments. This is still the dominant method for demonstrating tests' validity: often, test manuals simply report that the correlation beteen results obtained on the new test and results on some other popular test was such and such, without providing any reason why we should believe that the earlier test was valid. Kenneth Goodman (1973) has called this the 'sky-hook method' which ensures that new tests are anchored to old models of reading: 'If the new test is in fact measuring what the old test did, then why is a new test needed? And if the new test employs new insights, why expect it to correlate with the old?'

It's worth noting that human judgement is, at least in theory, the ultimate reference point in the validation of reading tests. Even if test constructors do not attempt to validate a new test with reference to assessments by professional teachers of reading, there is in principle some point at the beginning of the spiral where human judgement was consulted. In practice, very few test constructors carry out an exercise of cross-referencing with teachers' assessments as part of their validation procedures, because this dimension of validity is so problematical. On the one hand, many psychometricians object to the practice of consulting teachers, since it is the very subjectivity and inconsistency of teacher judgement which the tests aim to transcend. After all, test constructors would have a much more difficult time justifying their existence if tests merely reproduced teachers' assessments. On the other hand, even in cases where teacher judgement is treated as a legitimate standard of reference, the test constructor invariably defines the terms which will frame those judgements. Asking teachers to place children in rank order according to the teachers' estimate of their **reading age** is very different from asking teachers to convey their assessment of individual children as readers. In the first kind of consultation, test constructors are asking teachers to conform to a form of evaluation which has already been prescribed, i.e. the **reading age**. In the second, test constructors would be asking teachers to nominate a form of assessment which was compatible with their judgements and views of reading. Reports of validation procedures in test manuals never specify the extent to which teachers found the form of assessment employed in the test appropriate or consonant with their own judgement; they only report the extent to which the content of the assessments agreed. This leads directly into the third area of concern: the uses and understandings of the concept of **reading age**.

It is striking that in so many standard works on the assessment of reading we find reference made to the 'strong loyalty' commanded by the **reading age** amongst teachers (Vincent, 1974). Peter Pumfrey (1977) echoes this view:

> Teachers often find it helpful if a child's raw score on a reading test is converted to a reading age. *(p. 109)*

and

> Teachers are familiar with reading as a developmental process in which competence generally increases with age. Hence they are sympathetic towards the concept of reading ages. *(p. 111)*

In the main, this prevalent view is supported with evidence from surveys showing that the tests most commonly used by teachers are those which express their outcome in terms of **reading ages**.

It is interesting to observe that the use of the **reading age** as an index of children's overall scholastic performance grew rapidly during the period when the IQ was becoming discredited. We may speculate that **reading age** became a more politically acceptable index of aptitude than IQ because it appeared to express a generalised intellectual ability without the undesirable element of immutability which was associated with IQ. There is an interesting circularity in the use of **reading age** as an index of maturity/immaturity, since it has resulted from time to time in 'low **reading age**' being used as an explanation for poor reading performance!

It is worth asking why a normative, linear and age-related concept should persist in relation to reading, when it would not be acceptable in other areas of the curriculum. Is it because reading, unlike anything else taught in school, is still widely seen as skill and not knowledge, and therefore instrumental to the curriculum rather than an element of it? There is also reason to believe that **reading age** persists merely to ensure some continuity of comparability with the past: because **reading age** was the unit of currency used in the past, we still need it in order to compare 'standards over time', despite the many coherent and persuasive criticisms which have been made of the concept of **reading age**.

Finally, it should be acknowledged that the use of the **reading age** as a currency has probably declined in most professional contexts in recent years. In the UK, for example, the advent of the national curriculum and associated assessment arrangements have rendered the **reading age** somewhat obsolete. However, it must also be said that 'newer' models of reading assessment are underpinned by many of the same assumptions, despite their rhetorical commitment to 'criterion-referencing' and a more dynamic model of learning to read. The national curriculum for 'reading', for example, consists of ten levels of attainment, each tied to descriptors for the average child at particular ages. It is therefore based upon the same three theoretical assumptions which were described earlier in this entry in relation to the **reading age**.

If, for example, Level 2 can be used to categorise an average seven-year-old and a below-average eleven-year-old equally, and if normal children are expected to progress through one national curriculum level every two years, where is the difference between this and the **reading age**?

References
Ken Goodman (1973) 'Testing in reading: a general critique' in R.B. Ruddell (ed.) *Accountability and reading instruction: critical issues*. Illinois: National Council of Teachers of English.
Denis Vincent (1974) 'Reading ages and NFER tests'. *Educational Research 16*. No. 3, pp. 176–80.
Peter Pumfrey (1977) 'Reading measurement and evaluation: some current concerns' in J. Gilliland (ed.) *Reading: research and classroom practice*. London: Ward Lock Educational.

Reading schemes (also known as basals, readers and basal readers)

A **reading scheme** is a set of textbooks with reading passages of increasing difficulty designed specifically to teach reading. Although there are variations across **reading schemes** – some have more phonics, some have more literature, some more exercises, some more stories, some more subject-area passages – they are all based on the assumption that all children learn to read incrementally.

The use of **reading schemes** as reading pedagogy is widespread, so much so that for many no other way of teaching reading can even be imagined. Learning to read and making progress through a **reading scheme** have become synonymous. For many teachers and pupils it does not seem strange to have a reading textbook that is different from the book pupils are 'reading'; learning to read becomes divorced from 'reading'.

Although the use of **reading schemes** is widespread, there has been criticism: pupils often find the reading passages boring – the language of the reading passages is distorted and often more difficult to read than more naturally occurring language; pupils associate reading primarily with their textbooks, thus undervaluing the importance of reading beyond the **reading scheme**; teacher judgement and assessment are supplanted by the **reading scheme** (and by the tests that usually accompany **reading schemes**).

Reading schemes are a technology – a device, a 'machine' for teaching reading. Raw materials (children) inserted into one side of the technology are turned into products (readers) when they come out the other side. The only questions that are conventionally asked of technologies are questions of efficiency, so-called practical and managerial questions, for example: How fast do children become readers? How many children become readers? How many rejects are there? As a technology **reading schemes** take for granted questions of value: Of what value is reading to the children? What social and moral values are associated with how reading is implicitly defined? taught? conducted? with what is read?

However, **reading schemes** are not a neutral technology. In addition to having an implicit set of values and definitions of reading and of learning to read, **reading schemes** promote a set of social practices for reading. Some of these social practices include: grouping (grouping together all the pupils who have progressed to the same point in the **reading scheme**); waiting for the teacher to direct reading and to indicate successful reading; and abdicating authority to the technology to select what should be read, when, where, and how.

The introduction of **reading schemes** in the early twentieth century contributed to the evolution of classroom oral reading from a large-group, rote, and end-in-itself activity to a widely practised teaching and assessment technique based on small groups and one-to-one teacher–pupil interaction. As a collection of books designed to increase in difficulty in gradual increments, by means of carefully controlled vocabulary and complexity of language, the **reading scheme** achieved the dual status of method and material in teaching reading. Since **reading schemes** were devised according to the principle that a child will learn to read simply by making steady progress from one book to the next, and since beginning readers were not generally considered capable of silent reading, learning to read came to be seen as something directly dependent upon regular opportunities for children to read aloud from the **reading scheme**. With progress through the **reading scheme** so dependent upon frequent oral reading it is not surprising that oral reading soon became the cornerstone of conventional wisdom in reading pedagogy.

It is not just that **reading schemes** reflect a particular set of social practices; they also promote certain ways of using language. In the United States, where **reading schemes** are called basal readers, the term 'Basalese' was coined to designate the language of **reading schemes**. Basalese is a style of spoken language that closely follows the written language forms of a **reading scheme**. For example, consider the following passage from a **reading scheme**:[1]

> It is a **cat**.
> It is a **truck**.
> Is it a **can**? It is a **can**.[2]

Next to each sentence are a series of three pictures, one of which is the targeted word. For example, next to the first sentence, 'It is a **cat**', are pictures of a coat, a cat, and a tiger. The passage itself seems a simple matter of rendering the words aloud and matching the target word with the picture. But examine what happens when the passage is read in a reading group (/ marks indicate heavy stress intonation):

01 Teacher:	Okay	
02	Let's begin with Robin	
03	Read the first sentence, hun	
04 Robin:	It / is /	
05	It / is a / cat /	
06 Teacher:	Very good	

Robin reads the sentence in a halting manner, emphasising each word. Children often use this way of talking when they are pretending to read while playing school. But Basalese is not only a halting intonation pattern. It is also a manner of interacting with others and defining reading. Robin displays that she can render the words aloud. She displays this to the teacher and to her classmates. Her teacher responds by telling Robin that her reading was 'Very good'. Robin has 'successfully' performed the reading task. No one asks why they are reading the sentence, what the cat's name is – and if they were to ask such questions they would not be central to the lesson.

Basalese also occurs in the reading and comprehension of connected text. Henry had to respond to questions from the teacher about a story from the **reading scheme** being used in his reading group.

11 Teacher:	O.K. let's look at the picture
12	Where / is / the / cat / ?
13	Henry?
14 Henry:	On the on the truck
15 Teacher:	Complete sentence
16 Henry:	It / is / on / the / truck
17 Teacher:	O.K. Good

The teacher asked her question in Basalese, showing that Basalese is not just limited to children's language. Henry did not immediately respond in Basalese. He had to be reminded to do so and then he responded in Basalese and was told by the teacher that his performance was 'Good'.

Reading schemes, then, are not just a technology but a set of social and linguistic practices. There is a danger therefore in assuming that merely replacing **reading schemes** with different kinds of texts will by itself replace Basalese. Having learned Basalese, teachers and pupils do not need a **reading scheme** to speak it.

---

[1]This example is taken from D. Bloome and S. Neito (1989) 'Children's understandings of basal readers'. *Theory into Practice Vol. 28,* No. 4, pp. 258–64.

[2]The segment comes from William Durr, Jean LePere and Mary Lou Alsin (1979) *Rockets.* Boston, MA: Houghton Mifflin Company, p. 13 (a reading scheme book intended for year 1 pupils).

Real books

How does one distinguish **real books** from books that are not real? Many reading education programmes begin teaching children to read by using texts and stories designed to give pupils practice on various reading skills. The texts may be nonsense, such as 'The fat cat sat. Sat the fat cat', or may be designed to use only or nearly only the words children have already been taught. Often, the texts or books that young children are given to read as part of the reading education programme have been selected because of their readability level. Readability formulae often use word length (number of syllables) and sentence length (number of words) to calculate reading difficulty. As a result, in trying to make a reading passage with low readability which is presumably suitable for young children, the passages generally have short sentences and very limited and simple vocabulary. This often makes the passages awkward and, contrary to intent and expectation, more difficult to read either orally or for understanding. Perhaps just as significant is the tendency of reading programmes for young children to under-emphasise the importance of enjoying reading. Children need to learn not only how to read (how to render orally a text and how to understand it) but perhaps most importantly they need to learn the value of reading – how it can entertain them, how it can provoke their imagination, how it can make them reflect on their world, their family and themselves, how it can evoke emotions and feelings, and how it can be used to make friends and to learn and grow. Otherwise, reading is just empty-headed and heartless drudgery and work.

In response to the tendency of reading schemes and instructional programmes to emphasise reading passages for practice, skill and readability level, a number of reading researchers and teachers have argued for **real books** in reading education programmes, including and perhaps especially those for young children. They argued that young children and new readers (regardless of their age) were real readers too; they read for the same purpose as other more experienced readers and deserved to have books that would similarly be of interest and use to them. They further argued that there was a vast wealth of children's literature that could provide just the sort of books that children and new readers would enjoy and find engrossing.

But advocacy of **real books** has not been limited to supplementing the skills and practice orientation of reading education programmes. Rather, reading researchers and teachers argued that children *would learn to read* by reading **real books**. By learning to read by reading **real books**, they did not mean that children should be put in the middle of a pile of books and that they would learn to read. They meant a more active educational programme that helped connect children with **real books** by providing plenty of **real books**, by reading **real books** to them, by reading **real books** with them (both as a group and one-to-one), by having children write (real writing, not handwriting practice or spelling lists, but writing journals, stories and other real texts), by exploring words, sentences and other book features, and by a broad range of other instructional activities. In part, they based their advocacy for reading education based on **real books** on research that showed that reading is not learned one skill at a time. Indeed, it may be damaging to some children's long-term success as readers to learn one skill at a time. Instead, reading requires a broad range of strategies and skills that are used together, holistically, and children right from the very beginning can learn to read in a holistic manner. Further, research showed that the simplified and simplistic texts that children were often given as part of their reading instruction programmes were often harder to read because they lacked many of the textual features that help readers read and understand. Shortened sentences often fail to provide the connections between ideas because they lack various kinds of conjunctions (subordinators, relative clause markers, adverbial markers, among others). When shorter words are substituted for longer words, much of the meaning may be lost and the meaning may become vaguer and more abstract – often making the passage harder to understand and less interesting. When longer passages are shortened many of the cues that readers use to help them understand are lost. Especially important are redundancy cues. That is, meaning is not usually signalled just once in a passage or in just one way. A word or phrase may be rephrased or repeated. The syntax of a sentence and the overall structure of the text helps the reader refer back to previous meanings and may suggest again an earlier meaning or reference. When redundancy cues are eliminated – as often occurs when a passage is shortened or simplified – the text becomes harder to read and understand, not easier. Rather than simplifying books and texts for children and new readers to read, many researchers and educators advocated finding **real books** for them to read. Teachers could help children select **real books** that were of interest to them and that they would feel confident in using. And even if a book was 'too hard' for a child, they would probably be able to enjoy it and learn from it anyway, although in a different manner than a more experienced reader.

Thus **real books** does not really refer to **real books**, but to an approach and philosophy about the teaching of reading. But it is more than that. The debate over **real books** has been about whether **real books** approaches (there is not one approach but many) were more effective than the skill, drill and practice approaches. That debate continues, with each side claiming that research shows their approach to be best. Overshadowed by the debate on effectiveness is an important philosophical and political stance embedded in **real books**. Many of the people who advocate **real books** view children and new readers of whatever age as real readers. What this means is that children and new readers are entitled to be treated as a worthy audience in the same way as any other segment of the population. Real readers do not read books to learn to read; they read for a broad range of purposes and they read in a broad range of situations. By viewing children as real readers, advocates of **real books** take the stance that children should be treated with the same respect as other readers. This has profound implications for education and for how children are treated both in school and in society in general. It implies that children have intellectual depth and curiosity (perhaps not the same as adults but nonetheless as deep and as important) and that they have complex and legitimate emotions, values and objectives that cannot be dismissed merely because they are not adults. Not all advocates of **real books** maintain this stance; some view **real books** as just a more effective means to teach reading.

But can **real books** be distinguished from books that are not real? A few scholars and educators have suggested that the distinction between **real books** and others is problematical. They note that any activity in which a pupil engages is a real one, and any book or text they read is a real book or text. The book may not be one that the child enjoys reading and it may not be a book that many educators would describe as being of good quality, but it is a real book nonetheless even if it is just a book of nonsense drills. The debate here is different from the debate between **real books** advocates and skill, drill and practice advocates. The debate here is about recognising the complexity of the experiences children have in school, and that the experiences they have in school and especially in learning to read involve social and political issues, not just educational issues narrowly defined. Among the questions asked about **real books** from this perspective are: What are the cultural implications of a **real books** curriculum, especially for children who have been denied access to mainstream society? Does a **real books** curriculum privilege middle-class children and children from academically-orientated families? Does a curriculum so heavily focused on **real books** diminish other kinds of reading, writing and literacy? Does it promote one kind of social relationship at the expense of others? And is it not the case that at least some pupils enjoy reading the skill, drill and practice books and enjoy seeing themselves progress from level to level? Do not at least some pupils gain in confidence and self-concept through such reading programmes? Advocates of **real books** often see these questions as an attack on **real books** and as advocacy for skill, drill and practice. But the people who are asking questions like those above do not necessarily advocate skill, drill and practice – although some do. Many ask questions like those above in order to better understand the social, cultural and political dimensions of reading instruction, and are not advocating a particular approach to reading instruction.

Skill, drill and practice approaches to reading instruction can be measured. Statements can be made about how many skills a pupil has mastered, and what level of drill and practice they have advanced to. Of course, many people do not consider what is measured actually to be reading, especially not real reading. As stated in the Introduction, nominalisation of processes and actions (turning them into nouns) allows the process or action to be counted, measured, marketed and distributed.

Real reading is often treated as a verb and defies being counted, measured, marketed and distributed. But some teachers treat **real books**, which is often used as a synonym for real reading, as a noun. They count the number of **real books** their pupils have read and they may evaluate reading progress by the number of books read and the difficulty of the books read. In a different way, some politicians and educators have also used **real books** as a noun. They count the number of **real books** reading programmes in schools, and depending on their view, the more **real books** programmes there are the better or the worse. **Real books** reading programmes are marketed and distributed, sometimes by commercial enterprises and sometimes by public institutions. Whether the nominalisation of **real books**, as a synonym for real reading, is a good thing or a bad thing, depends on how the counting, measuring, marketing and distributing are done, for what purpose, and on one's point of view and political interests. But it is useful to ask the question: What would the consequences be if **real books** were not treated as a noun?

Remedial reading

Remedial reading is often defined in standard reading education textbooks as special teaching or a special reading programme given to pupils who are more than two years below their peers' average reading level. Notice that the definition of **remedial reading** is not a definition of reading *per se,* but is both a definition of the pupil as reader and a definition of an educational programme for **remedial readers.** The pupil who is not able to read the same books and texts as her or his same-age peers, whose reading age (see **Reading age**) is below that of the others, becomes a **remedial reader** and is given a specialised reading programme to accommodate the pupil's condition.

Typically, **remedial readers** are identified through diagnostic tests. The diagnosis may include labelling and identification of specific skills the pupil lacks or the cognitive processes the pupil fails to engage in. For example, the pupil may lack the ability to identify medial vowels, or to blend letter-sounds together, or to identify the main idea of a passage, or to distinguish fact from opinion. Or the pupil may lack various metacognitive and metalinguistic skills, such as assuming a purpose for reading a passage, knowing what an index is, knowing what a sentence is, self-correcting as needed. However, the term **remedial reader** is not limited to those children identified through tests. The term may also be used to refer to any pupil who is not reading as well as expected, as in 'John is really a **remedial reader**; he has a hard time reading the textbook'.

Being a **remedial reader** is both an educational label and a social identity, as in 'We need to test the children in this classroom to identify the **remedial readers** so we can earmark them for the **remedial reading** programme' and 'Sally is a **remedial reader**; she doesn't get much support at home'.

The terms **remedial reading** and **remedial reader** require the support of a large number of other concepts – reading age, reading levels, reading skills, reading diagnosis, skill deficiencies and readers who are not **remedial** – as well as an extensive technology – standardised tests, diagnostic tests, skill sequences and hierarchies. Thus, to use the term **remedial reading** or **remedial reader** is to invoke the large number of other concepts associated with them as well as associated technologies, and to assume the validity of those concepts and the technology. In many ways, therefore, the concepts of **remedial reading** and **remedial reader** are fragile concepts. If one of the related concepts or if part of the technology breaks down, the whole of **remedial reading** shatters.

But the questions to ask about **remedial reading** and **remedial readers** are not just about the validity of the concepts themselves or of the concepts associated with them; questions need to be asked about what ideological work the concepts of **remedial reading** and **remedial reader** do. One way to get at this is to ask: What are the opposites of **remedial reading** and **remedial reader**? They don't really have opposites in the sense that there is not a special name for pupils who are two years ahead of their peers in reading age. They might be called gifted readers, or early readers if they are young children, but those terms are rarely used and seem more like opposites of terms such as 'developmentally delayed pupil' than **remedial reader**. And what kind of reading programme would be the opposite of a **remedial reading** programme? An advanced reading programme? Perhaps, but such a term is rarely used, even if some pupils are given advanced books to read. Rather, the opposite of **remedial reading** is the *ordinary and usual reading education programmes that ordinary and usual pupils receive*. The terms **remedial reading** and **remedial reader** work as exclusion categories while at the same time protecting the ordinary and usual reading education programmes as well as the educational identity of the ordinary and usual pupils – they are defined as being *not* **remedial readers**.

The ideological work done by the terms **remedial reading** and **remedial reader** is also highlighted if we define them within an unfamiliar context. For example, consider the terms and new definitions below:

A remedial reading programme is a reading education programme that does not promote the reading growth and development of all pupils at a rate that is at least adequate to the academic expectations made of them and at a level of their interest and desire.

Such a definition would shift the stigma from the pupils to the reading education programme ordinarily and usually provided.

A remedial reader is a pupil who has to learn to read in a remedial reading programme (new definition above).

This new definition shifts the stigma from the pupil to the conditions within which the pupil must learn to read, and in so doing negates the exclusion category generated by the old definitions of **remedial reading** and **remedial reader**.

Of course, neither new definition is likely to catch on, since what drives the terms **remedial reading** and **remedial reader** is not a linguistic issue but a need to justify the ordinary and usual reading education programmes provided and to rationalise both the exclusion of some pupils and the privileges accorded to others.

Skills (Reading skills)

There is something appealing and common-sensical about **skills**. The word conjures up notions of basic practical know-how. However, having **skills** is different from being skilled. **Skills** are things, which you either have or haven't got, or are in the process of getting. **Skills** are things which some people have got and others haven't got. **Skills** are, for the most part, rudimentary things ('cooking **skills**', 'driving **skills**'), whereas when we say that someone is *skilled* we imply not only that they are able to do something in a particular field of endeavour, but moreover that they are especially good at it, that they are something of an expert (a 'skilled cook', a 'skilled driver'). Skilled people can be contrasted with the 'semi-skilled' and the 'unskilled'. **Skills** therefore works metaphorically to evoke the discourse of the market-place and the labour market: **skills** are distributed to individuals, acquired by individuals and traded by individuals for jobs, goods and services.

In contemporary educational circles, the connotations of the term **skills** are somewhat contradictory. On the one hand, the term has progressive, child-centred associations, especially when contrasted with knowledge. In the discourse of curriculum studies, knowledge in a school subject consists of the decontextualised content of the subject – the product – and **skills** refers to the ability to apply knowledge, to practise and deploy the range of competences associated with the subject – in other words, the process. In science, for example, it is possible to contrast the vast amount of scientific knowledge, which is often only learned by tedious memorisation and assessed through formal examinations, with the scientific **skills** of, for example, investigation, problem-solving, team-work and the evaluation of evidence.

On the other hand, **skills** take on colder, more mechanistic overtones when they are thought of as the component parts of a competence which is generally seen as unified – or at least complex and made up of many interrelated abilities – and which has been broken down into discrete parts and then described, taught and assessed as separate skills. The kinds of competences which seem especially vulnerable to this kind of fragmentation are ordinary everyday behaviours: socialising is broken down into 'social **skills**'; communicating into 'communication **skills**'; thinking into 'thinking **skills**'; even living into 'life **skills**'. This kind of splitting-up is given credence by the growth in prestige of behavioural objectives approaches in various training programmes, especially in industry, where each of the intended outcomes of training (which may in some contexts be useful as frameworks for understanding, assessing or describing competences) have been adopted as separate elements in a syllabus. They are then often taught with very little consideration given to how they relate to each other.

In discourse terms, it is probably the use of the plural form which makes a term like **reading skills** especially problematical. The plural form signifies a lack of integration and unity: it denotes something very different from 'reading *skill*' in the singular form, or '*skill* in reading' (evoking images of a 'skilled reader'), or even 'aspects of the reading *skill*'. The term **reading skills** works discursively in much the same way as the terms 'social **skills**' or 'communication **skills**', in that it takes for granted the need to separate the larger, rather mysterious, competence into its component parts in order to understand it and help people to get better at it. Within the dominant discourse of reading pedagogy, **reading skills** represents a self-evidently sensible way of understanding the process of reading and learning to read. **Reading skills** are the things which novice readers are taught, and which improve as they become better readers. These might be, for example, specific processes of 'phonetic analysis', or 'comprehension', or 'aesthetic appreciation', or 'information retrieval'. Owning 'good' **reading skills** is an essential part of being a fully-fledged adult, part of the basic kit, just like good social **skills** and good communication **skills**.

The fundamental problem with the notion of **reading skills** is that it functions discursively to convince us that an analysis of what readers do (their behaviour) is the same thing as an analysis of how novice readers *learn* and how they should be taught. It positions any alternative pedagogy as anti-common sense. To illustrate this danger with a deliberately extreme example: it's one thing to say that 'skilled' readers' eyes move in particular ways as they read; it is quite another thing to set out to teach people to move their eyes in that way. This is the danger of adopting **skills** (which are useful ways of understanding the outcomes of teaching or aspects of competence) as teaching objectives.

Standards (Reading standards)

Standard is a term of comparison or exclusion: it is used when comparing one thing or person with another, one group with another, one thing or person in relation to a larger group, one period of time with another, one place with another. The irony is that, even in its conventional everyday usage – leaving aside for the moment its position within educational discourse – it is used to express many different kinds of comparison or exclusion. Some of them actually contradict others. For example:

1.   We use **standard** to mean a hurdle, a minimum level of acceptability, as in 'you have failed to meet the **standard** required for admission to the programme'.

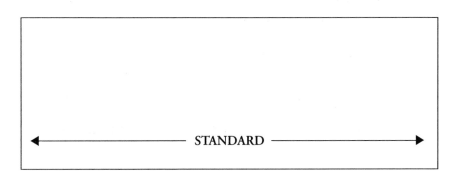

2.   We use **standard** to represent a degree of excellence: 'As you might expect in an hotel of this calibre, The Bismark has **standards**, and this is a source of some pride'.

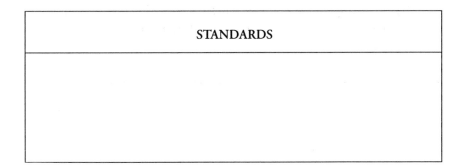

3.   We use **standard** to express regularity and uniformity, as in 'our quality control procedures assure you a **standard** product every time'.

STANDARD	STANDARD	STANDARD
STANDARD	STANDARD	STANDARD
STANDARD	STANDARD	STANDARD
STANDARD	STANDARD	STANDARD

4.   We use **standard** to denote prevalence, or normality, or commonality, as in 'the **standard** opinion among most people was that he was guilty'.

NONSTANDARD	STANDARD	NONSTANDARD

5.   We use **standard** to imply ordinariness, or a fairly rudimentary level, strongly implying a superior version elsewhere: 'For customers with a limited budget, we suggest the 1.1 L, the **standard** product in the range', and, more recently, 'The restaurant car is open to both **Standard** Class and First Class customers'.

STANDARD

6.   We use **standard** to assign a value, grade or rate to something such as a
      performance, behaviour or outcome: 'The **standards** of this team are
      appalling' or 'They enjoy a high **standard** of living'.

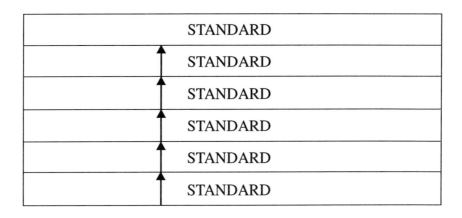

Despite their differences, each of these meanings evoke images of measurement,
accuracy, grades of quality, industrial production and competitive evaluation. It's
worth mentioning in passing that, with such a proliferation of sometimes
contradictory meanings associated with one word, it's astonishing that we aren't more
confused than we are by people's use of the term. However, when a term with such a
complex web of meanings is used within the culture of education, in as volatile an
area as reading, and generally in highly-charged and politically sensitive debates over
the success or failure of children, teachers and the system as a whole, it is hardly
surprising that it has assumed a position of contest – symbolically, and in practice.

We might learn more about how the term **standards** functions within the discourse
of reading pedagogy if we apply the six meanings delineated above to the specific
context of reading. By doing so, we can see that:

1.   **Reading standards** can mean minimum or threshold levels of competence
      for an age group, or for promotion to a more advanced level or group.

2.   **Reading standards** can be used to refer to the consistently excellent reading
      performance or level expected of a particular individual or group.

3.   **Reading standards** implies **standard** readers, each equipped with identical
      resources with only a minimal tolerance for variation between them.

4.   Although the term is not generally used in this sense, **reading standard** can be used to refer to the kind and level of reading that most people do: a **standard reading.** The linguistic parallel is standard English: the (supposedly) prevalent and widely-used form, the form that brings one into the mainstream, the currency which is most readily accepted and exchanged. In this sense, **reading standard/standard reading** implies **standard** texts, and **standard readings** of those texts. And so it is not especially fanciful to detect in the term **reading standards** a notion of 'cultural literacy' (cf. Hirsch, 1987) which privileges the established canon of heritage texts over 'non-standard' texts, and which assumes a monolithic correct reading of those texts, thus excluding the possibility of alternative readings which draw on the reader's cultural, historical and linguistic resources.

5.   Here again, although not generally used in this sense, **reading standards** can be used to refer to a basic, rudimentary or functional level of reading, by implication distinguishing it from the superior version. In this sense, **reading standard** can imply **standard reading** *competence*, as in 'standard equipment'.

6.   **Reading standards** can be stages of reading proficiency, each successive step requiring greater competence. The image is of a very narrow staircase: developmental, linear, hierarchical and one-dimensional.

The additional dimension to these meanings in the discourse of reading pedagogy, which gives the term **standards** such a high charge, is that the term is generally used when referring to *change over time*: the syntax tends to combine the subject **reading standards** with the verb *have fallen/risen*. However, as we can see from the earlier examination of meanings associated with the term **reading standards**, there is an in-built ambiguity in any such claim, since some meanings are linked to movement in the calibration (meanings 1, 2 and 3), while others refer to movement in performance (meanings 4, 5 and 6). If some change over time is being claimed, wherein lies the change? Is it in the definitions, or expectations, or thresholds by which **reading standard**-ness is met, or is it in the performance of the readers? If the claim is that **standards** have risen or fallen, does this mean that children's reading has remained constant but the expectation/calibration has changed, or that the expectation/calibration has remained constant but children's reading has changed?

During the 1980s the term **standards** became a critical element in the educational discourse adopted by political lobbyists attempting to persuade central government in Britain to re-vamp its educational policy along 'market-led' and 'consumerist' lines, with such features as national tests, school vouchers, greater selection and so on. The British government eventually embraced this ideology and committed itself to 'raising **standards**' through such measures as a national curriculum, national tests, performance league tables, open enrolment and so on. We may note in passing a certain congruence of metaphors here: the only major political party in Britain which explicity identifies itself with the British flag (the 'Union Jack'), thereby claiming the status of '**standard** bearer', has nailed its colours to the rhetoric of 'raising **standards**'.

Reference
[1]E.D. Hirsch (1987) *Cultural literacy: what every American needs to know.* Boston MA: Houghton Mifflin.

Word attack

Attack derives from the generative metaphor of *War*.

> *The Metaphor:* THE WAR
>
> *What it generates:* STRUGGLE
>
> *Universe as war:* The triumph of being over nothingness.
>> The battlefield.
>
> *Society as war.* The subjection of weak to strong.
>
> *Person as warrior:* Courage; the hero.
>> *Medicine* as victory over death.
>
> *Mind as warrior:* Conquistador.
>> *Language as* control.
>
> *The relationship of human with other beings in war.* Enmity.
>
> *Images of the War.* Victory, defeat, loot, ruin, the army.

from Ursula Le Guin (1986)
Always coming home
London: Victor Gollancz Ltd, p. 483

NOT THE LAST WORD

The title of this last section is an obvious play on 'words', allowing us to signal several meanings simultaneously and to offer several invitations. As we noted in the Introduction, there are other key terms in the teaching of reading, in addition to the twenty-four here, that need to be examined, unpacked for their ideological assumptions and for the subtle ways they influence what we do in the teaching of reading. New words and terms are constantly being invented or borrowed from other fields or from everyday life and imported into the teaching of reading. We need to examine these other terms and how they are used; the title of this postscript is in part an invitation and encouragement to do so.

Of course, it is not just words that need to be examined. The *styles* of language used in the field, the 'scientific' and 'professional' clothing that the language of the teaching of reading occasionally wears, also need to be scrutinised. We need to examine when and where such styles of language happen, what meanings are suggested, and what 'work' is being accomplished. We have pointed to some influences that the 'grammar' of the professional language of teaching reading may have; for example the influence of nominalisation. But we have done little more than hint at the importance of examining how the 'grammar' of the field influences the way we conceptualise teaching, reading and learning.

Another meaning of our title, 'Not the last word', is an acknowledgment that we do not claim to have 'the last word' on any of the key terms we have discussed. We invite you to re-examine the words we have discussed in this book. Some people may disagree with how we have discussed or critiqued a particular term. They may feel we have over-emphasised one dimension at the expense of others or that we have entirely missed an important point. In our defence, we can only state that we have not attempted to write definitive entries on any of the key terms in this book. We have varied our approaches to the key terms in order to show a broad range of approaches that might be used to examine the key terms in our field. And, we are aware that the language we have used in discussing key terms is itself open to ideological critique. Thus we view the entries in this book as the beginning of what could be – and should be – a long and continuing conversation among teachers, teacher educators, scholars and anyone interested in the teaching of reading.

There are those who will wonder what the purpose of this critique is. They may wonder if it is just an academic exercise. Perhaps as worrisome are those who will conclude from our critique that we are suggesting that there is no knowledge and no substance in the field of reading.

With regard to the latter, there are of course many kinds and sources of knowledge: knowledge that comes from the experiences of teachers and pupils, knowledge that comes from scholarly studies and knowledge that is generated through debate. As a field – and like any healthy field – we are constantly arguing about the nature of knowledge in our field. What counts as knowledge? How particularistic and how general is the knowledge we have? (Does it apply only in certain contexts or does it extend across a broad range of contexts?) How are we using the knowledge we have and how could we use it? How should we generate new knowledge? The words and language we use to talk about teaching and reading influence our stance towards knowledge in the field, and therefore how we answer the questions above. The words and language we use make it seem common-sensical and natural to act in particular ways, to approach the teaching of reading in a particular manner. By critiquing the key terms in the field, we are able to question what seems common-sensical and natural, and to open up new possibilities for understanding and teaching reading. The opening up of new possibilities is one answer to the charge that the critique of key terms is merely an academic exercise.

A second answer focuses on the exercise of authority in the teaching of reading. Many of us feel that, increasingly, our authority and ability to act on our own best judgement have been and continue to be eroded. Some of that erosion comes from politicians who want to exert increased control over what happens in schools. Some of the erosion comes from packaged teaching programmes that require teachers to follow step-by-step instructions or from administrators who demand a particular teaching regimen. We rightly question such distanced authority and control, and argue that we – as teachers, teacher educators and researchers – should be allowed to exercise our professional judgement. Yet, we often overlook the distanced authority and control that is exerted by the key terms and language of the field itself. Just as politicians attempt to constrain the options we might employ in our teaching, and the educational futures we might create for our pupils, by restructuring resources, promulgating rules and setting the terms of the national debate on education, so too the vocabulary and language of the teaching of reading orientates us to particular ways of thinking and ways of acting.

Our critique in this book is intended to challenge the distanced authority and influence of the key terms in the teaching of reading. Therefore, we have not suggested an alternative set of terms to replace those we have critiqued – even those key terms that we have found, in our opinion, to have damaging influences. That would merely supplant one distanced authority with another. Rather, we hope we have made it difficult for any set of key terms to exert influence and authority over the teaching of reading without being subjected to constant critique and interrogation. And, we hope we have made it easier for everyone involved in the teaching of reading – teachers, teacher educators, researchers, parents, administrators and pupils – to participate in that critique.